16 HOUSES

16 HOUSES

DESIGNING THE PUBLIC'S PRIVATE HOUSE MICHAEL BELL

THE MONACELLI PRESS

For my family

First published in the United States of America in 2003 by
The Monacelli Press, Inc.
902 Broadway, New York, New York 10010

Library of Congress Cataloging-in-Publication Data
16 houses : designing the public's private house / [edited by] Michael Bell.
    p.   cm.
Includes bibliographical references.
ISBN 1-58093-114-6
1. Low-income housing—Texas—Houston. 2. Housing subsidies—Texas—Houston. 3. Architecture, Domestic—Texas—Houston. I. Title: Designing the public's private house. II. Title: Sixteen houses. III. Bell, Michael (Michael J.).
HD7287.96.U62T415   2003

363.5'8'097641411—dc21   2003012356

Printed and bound in Italy

Editor: Chuihua Judy Chung
Designer: Sze Tsung Leong

Photographers: Deron Neblett (Fifth Ward photography), Ben Thorne (exhibition photography)
Production Assistants: Christopher Chew and Ruben Jackson

Editor for The Monacelli Press: Noel Millea

16 Houses Program and Exhibition
Michael Bell, Founder and Director
Mardie Oakes, Assistant Curator, Project Manager, Fifth Ward Community Redevelopment Agency (1995–2000)
Emily Todd, Executive Director, DiverseWorks Artspace (1995–99)
Anna Mod, Project Manager, Fifth Ward Community Redevelopment Agency
Diane Barber, Visual Arts Director, DiverseWorks Artspace
Keith Krumwiede, Assistant Curator, Assistant Professor, Rice University School of Architecture

Exhibition Design: Michael Bell and Kerry Whitehead
Display Tables: Kerry Whitehead
Entryway Design and Graphics: Gunar Hartmann and Logan Ray

Funding for 16 Houses was provided by:
Graham Foundation for Advanced Studies in the Fine Arts
DiverseWorks Artspace
Fifth Ward Community Redevelopment Corporation of Houston
Cultural Arts Council of Houston and Harris Counties
Local Initiatives Support Corporation of New York
Bank United
Rice University School of Architecture
Columbia University Graduate School of Architecture, Planning, and Preservation
anonymous donors

Contents

Acknowledgments

There are many people whose efforts made *16 Houses* a success. Foremost is Emily Todd, then–executive director of DiverseWorks Artspace, who offered the prospect of an exhibition. By supporting the project during its research phase, she provided the commitment that encouraged others to join us. Mardie Oakes, then–project manager at the Fifth Ward Community Redevelopment Corporation, bridged theory and practice, making the connection between architectural academia and community and grassroots redevelopment, and in the process redefining both—as she did her role as assistant curator, client, and fund-raiser. Stephen Fairfield and Kathy Payton of the Fifth Ward Community Redevelopment Corporation contributed to the project's sense of purpose and longevity, as did Anna Mod. Lars Lerup gave support in the first stage. Jessica Cusick of the Cultural Arts Council of Houston and Harris Counties challenged us to incorporate wider-ranging influences from the arts community. Doris Anderson, Elaine Sebring, Kathleen Roberts, Diania Williams, and Janet Wheeler from the Rice School of Architecture helped to bring together sixteen architects from across the United States. Gunar Hartmann and Logan Ray were instrumental in designing the exhibition's entry hall. Keith Krumwiede also assisted in the design of the installation and determining the roster of architects. At DiverseWorks Artspace, Diane Barber provided support and insight, especially during the installation. Kerry Whitehead managed the installation of the sixteen works and almost single-handedly welded and installed the tables on which they were displayed. Her subtle design work is evident throughout the exhibition.

The advisory committee included Reverend Harvey Clemons, president of the FWCRC board of directors; Robert Toliver, builder and Fifth Ward resident; Stephen Fox of the Anchorage Foundation, Houston; Aaron Betsky, director of the Netherlands Architecture Institute; Farés El Dahdah, professor at the Rice School of Architecture; and Jeff Balloutine, vice president for community reinvestment at Bank United. The committee helped formulate plans to build a selection of the houses.

In New York, Terence Riley offered early advice and continued support by opening the Museum of Modern Art archives to share curatorial notes from MoMA housing exhibitions. At Columbia, Bernard Tschumi, Gwendolyn Wright, and Laurie Hawkinson created an environment that allowed these ideas to flourish. Kenneth Frampton, Steven Holl, Stan Allen, Mary McLeod, Richard Plunz, Scott Marble, Karen Fairbanks, Karla Rothstein, Kathryn Dean, Mark Rakatansky, Robert Marino, Charles Eldred, and especially Grant Marani all offered new insight as the project evolved during the school's long-running housing studio. Peggy Deamer, Robert Stern, Toshiko Mori, Jorge Silvetti, Michael Hays, Dana Cuff, Sylvia Lavin, Kevin Alter, Gary Paige, Karrie Jacobs, Reed Kroloff, and Cathy Ho offered new venues to discuss the work. Bruce Mau also gave encouragement and support, and Shaila Dewan contributed two critical texts.

Deron Neblett responded to a call to create a photographic journal of the Fifth Ward, and his portraits of local residents revealed the vitality of the neighborhood.

Mark Wamble, Sanford Kwinter, Albert Pope, Carlos Jiménez, Stanley Saitowitz, and Aaron Betsky continually provided inspiration and friendship. Special thanks go to Ruben Jackson and Chris Chew, who assisted in this book, and to Todd Vanvarick and John Mueller. Thanks also to Chuihua Judy Chung and Sze Tsung Leong, whose talent, clarity, and insight are seen in the editing and design—again—and to Gianfranco Monacelli, Andrea Monfried, and Noel Millea for tremendous support.

The most important recognition goes to the students, whose energy, enthusiasm, and talent continually renew architecture.

Designing the Public's Private House

Michael Bell

Architecture = Policy

Owning a House in the City

In 1996, the Clinton administration's plan to reduce the concentration of public housing in city centers was accelerated by the allocation of federal funding for housing vouchers. Intended to encourage property ownership among a wide spectrum of lower-income Americans, vouchers provide a onetime subsidy at the time of sale—in effect, supplying a down payment for the buyer. In 1998, the Quality Housing and Work Responsibility Act augmented this effort.[1] These initiatives were both pragmatic and ideological, dealing with issues of poverty, the deconstruction of the racial and ethnic territories created by previous federal housing programs, and historic urban paradigms of density and centripetal concentration.

Between 1996 and 2001, as U.S. federal housing policy moved toward relying on voucher programs that enabled public-private partnerships to produce more of the country's low-income housing, more than fifty-one thousand public housing rental units were razed or converted to subsidized private housing.[2] In most cases, these efforts were successful, and former tenants of low-income apartments were relocated to traditional single-family houses, low-rise housing blocks, condominiums, and townhouses dispersed throughout urban centers.

16 Houses: Designing the Public's Private House examines the architectural implications of this dispersal. It represents the work of architects and theoreticians who participated in *16 Houses: Owning a House in the City*, an ongoing, multifaceted redevelopment project for Houston's Fifth Ward Community Redevelopment Corporation. Pragmatically, *16 Houses* focuses on the urgent need for inventive lower-income housing. Theoretically, it addresses the issue of decentralization in relation to a range of spatial, economic, racial, and ultimately technical concerns. And, perhaps most important, it focuses on the role architecture has played in relation to the highly politicized issues of housing, poverty, and race since the 1930s.

The sixteen architects were asked to examine how a "voucher house"—a term the architects used during the design process without a great deal of scrutiny—could fulfill its role in influencing the creation of new quasi-market-rate housing policy. They were provided with practical and theoretical information that made the work specific to Houston and the Fifth Ward, a predominantly African American neighborhood in downtown Houston with the city's lowest average household income,[3] and they were asked to respond within spatial and technical parameters that were architectural and tectonic in nature. They were also asked to respond to issues of subjectivity in regard to the power relations historically embedded in U.S. housing policy.

In their private practices, the architects had all explored the relationship between architecture and contemporary urbanism, and in most cases, they also taught in schools where urbanism and architecture merge around themes of territory and power. Though there are divisions between planning and architecture in many universities, in this project the two fields by necessity inflect each other and at times fuse.[4] The sixteen had already examined the urban and architectural fragmentation that often results from development of market-rate housing in the United States, and had attempted to avoid these pitfalls in private practice, often with great success. Yet most of them had not dealt with low-income housing or its relationship to issues of race, income, territory, and federal policy.

The goal was to bring to this realm of development a renewed theory of architecture and urbanism and a critical theory of the city in relation to power and territory. In this study, the single-family house is the end product of the voucher program. It's also evidence that invention can serve as a node or fragment of a larger political and urban agenda.

The Fifth Ward in Data (Fifth Ward = 3,192 acres, or five square miles)

| | Fifth Ward | | Houston | |
	1990	2000	1990	2000
Total Population	21,899	23,921	1,630,533	1,941,240
Non-Hispanic Whites	1%	2%	41%	29%
Non-Hispanic Blacks	79%	67%	27%	24%
Hispanics	20%	30%	28%	39%
Asians	0%	1%	4%	5%
Education				
No diploma	43%	43%	30%	27%
High school diploma	30%	42%	22%	19%
College degree	4%	7%	21%	18%
Graduate studies	1%	4%	9%	10%
Age				
65 and over	15%	14%	8%	8%
Employment				
Employed	38%	34.4%	63%	64%
Unemployed	11%	7.3%	5%	6.6%
Not in labor force	51%	58.3%	50%	45%
Per capita income		$8,450		$42,598

Source: City of Houston Department of Planning and Development, *Super Neighborhood Resource Assessment* (Houston, 1999)

Background

The federal funds made available in 1996 for down-payment voucher programs augmented financial incentives already in place for public-private partnerships in housing development—historic-preservation and low-income tax credits, tax abatements, and donated city land. This combination of incentives has sometimes influenced design decisions: historic-preservation tax credits are often coupled with low-income housing tax credits in a way that lowers development costs while mandating historical housing types. In most cases, however, these incentives have no clear architectural or urban expression, and the development processes usually result in typical speculative housing, with low-level building and design practices.

Voucher programs have moved the point of entry of subsidies to strategic junctures in the development process: the funding arrives when the house is sold, well after the design process is complete, which has had the de facto effect of eliminating the professional services of architects. The housing is essentially market-rate, and the design process virtually nonexistent. *16 Houses* was initiated, in part, because the appearance of most subsidized housing reflects this elimination of the design process—and fails to reflect the complexity of the political and economic forces at play in the development of housing and the organization of the contemporary city.

The research that laid the groundwork for *16 Houses* has continued beyond the initially planned exhibition and publication. Thanks to funding from the Local Initiatives Support Corporation of New York, six of the houses are now in working drawings, and one of them has been built and sold. Collectively, these houses demonstrate the means by which political and economic power is revealed or concealed in architectural design. Most of the architects were as preoccupied with the labor processes involved in construction as they were with spatial and programmatic goals. The agency of architecture was also an important concern: each architect—and the project at large—addresses the issue of how the designs exert power in their own right, or function as an adjunct to other forms of power.

Decentralization

Decentralization—on a practical level and as a political concern—proved to be the most enduring issue. While the architectural designs stand alone, and ultimately must operate on a pragmatic level, the question of political consequence remains. *16 Houses* treads a line between supporting the effort to move federal housing initiatives toward the market and critiquing the substandard quality of market-rate housing in the United States. The projects outline goals and techniques for a type of housing that offers an alternative to the concentration, isolation, and segregation that characterize much federal housing design, while recognizing that market practices have yet to produce an obvious high-quality alternative.

16 Houses is useful as a set of practical proposals, but its real value lies in the degree to which the entire project and the individual works emerged from applying architectural principles to public policy—the projects are literal volumetric and tectonic responses to policy goals. Themes of centrifugal and centripetal space[5] as characteristic of urban form and housing policy—of decentralization—become both practical and symbolic. This group of architects begins what may be a generational movement toward renewing the political purpose of architectural space and production.

None of the works seeks to revive a particular historical genre or form of architecture. Many of the architects rely on a vocabulary of modern architecture, but none focuses on syntactical or formal transformations as a mode of autonomy or self-reference. Several of these architects learned formal syntax as well as transformational strategies from works by John Hejduk and Peter Eisenman (particularly from the publication *Five Architects*), yet in their careers they have opened their work to a broader negotiation of themes of territory and power, and in most cases, this opening has diminished the formal clarity of the works.

16 Houses is steeped in the idea of resistance: the works highlight the unresolved urban and political crisis in housing and, more broadly, address the construction and legislation of social, racial, and economic territories in housing. The project doesn't attempt to reinvent grassroots political action or the forms of litigation that accompany contentious housing development, but it does test the potential of resistance and engagement under the current conditions of U.S. building practices.

Between 1996 and 1998, the genesis of this approach can be seen in brief passages in essays by Sanford Kwinter and K. Michael Hays. Regarding resistance, Kwinter, in his "Far From Equilibrium" column in *ANY,* described anyone who "still" relied on the "efficacy of negative dialectics" as "gullible."[6] Hays's introduction to *Architecture Theory Since 1968* concluded that a younger audience may have such an "altogether altered" relationship to consumption that its members had become hesitant to engage in a practice that resisted the dominant productive economies of the city. Hays suggested that an overt resistance to the commodity processes of labor, material, and financing, which underlie the production of architecture, may no longer hold appeal for younger architects.[7] His coda, unlike Kwinter's, affirms the role of negative dialectics in the face of a significant political and productive crisis, but concludes that the sustained expansion of the United States economy affected the degree to which a new generation sought refuge against the market. The pliability of the formal work in *16 Architects* reflects this condition: the architects were working between modes of engagement and resistance, and the houses in turn reveal the strife of their origins.

Similar themes were the basis of *Slow Space,* a book I coedited with Sze Tsung Leong. *Slow Space* measured the local, small-scale, volumetric, and tectonic ambitions of architecture—for instance, John Hejduk's Bye House—against the fluid and global processes of urban finance, trade, and labor. It characterized Houston as an emblematic postwar U.S. city with formal and architectural attributes that have become increasingly fragmented and visually inchoate as its financial, media, and production systems have become unified and virtually self-perpetuating. The goal was, and still is, to view architecture as being enzymatically sustained rather than undermined by urban processes of rationalization, production, and finance—yet also to promote the role of resistance. Each of the works in *16 Houses* exhibits both positions. Procedural and temporal ideas of architectural and urban production—systems of management, legislation, and finance, and the role of the state as it protects the market—are given architectural presence.

Ever Modern

16 Houses situates architecture at a historic transition between socialist and free-market interpretations of United States federal housing policy. In the first wave of federal housing in the 1930s, public housing was often considered a form of socialism; the government was thought to be subverting market processes with its housing policy. However, the homogeneity of the public housing population (in terms of race, gender, and income) has continually undermined the classless aspirations that imbued social housing in Europe.

In his introduction to *Five Architects*, Colin Rowe derided American modernism for being devoid of clear "political pedigree," contending that in Europe, modern architecture was an adjunct to socialism, ideologically rooted in Marxism. In other words, it is not clear that public housing was *ever* ideologically modern in the United States, even if its forms appeared to be so. *16 Houses*, a collection of small-scale projects, emerges from this momentous juncture in which quasi-socialist ideologies are becoming quasi-market ideologies, and competing histories and procedures are threatening as well as enabling work on behalf of an impoverished constituency.

Timeline

Three Phases, Five Years, Sixteen Houses

Part exhibition, part building program, part research project, and most important, a collective work of architecture and planning, *16 Houses* developed in three distinct phases. Each stage relied on the expertise of new participants and was funded by different sources.

I founded *16 Houses* in 1995 with a grant from the Graham Foundation of Chicago; the first three years consisted of a study of the economics and design of the single-family house and its pivotal role in down-payment voucher programs initiated by the federal government. The primary goal was to examine the architectural implications of the new federal policy of decentralization and dispersal.

In April 1998, sixteen architects were invited to assemble teams to design single-family houses for the Fifth Ward Community Redevelopment Corporation in Houston. Financial supporters included DiverseWorks Artspace, Rice University, and Bank United. Architects who chose to work with an artist, a writer, or another design professional also received funding from the Cultural Arts Council of Houston and Harris Counties. Assisting with the direction of the project were Mardie Oakes, project manager for the FWCRC, Emily Todd, executive director of DiverseWorks, and Keith Krumwiede of the Rice University School of Architecture.

An exhibition of the projects, *16 Houses: Owning a House in the City,* opened on November 6, 1998, at DiverseWorks in Houston. More than a thousand people crowded the gallery on opening night. Over six hundred invitations were sent to Fifth Ward residents in addition to the nine hundred people on the DiverseWorks mailing list. Two community events supported the exhibition: a midday discussion with the designers for area students and a panel discussion, held on December 12, 1998, with guests from the community, including Bank United vice president for community reinvestment Jeff Balloutine. In the spring of 1999, the exhibition moved to the University of Texas at Austin.

The third phase started in 2000, when a selection committee chose seven of the sixteen projects to be built. Funding from the Local Initiatives Support Corporation of New York allowed the FWCRC to move closer to construction by providing professional fees for contract documents for each project. At this point, the house designed by Morris Gutierrez Architects is complete, and six others are ready for construction on sites purchased by the FWCRC.

Voucher House

Public Housing Becomes Voucher House

The history of public housing in Houston began in 1938 with the formation of the Housing Authority of the City of Houston (HACH). Funded by the United States Housing Authority, HACH was created as part of the New Deal housing reform, and was controversial from its inception. Home builders and savings-and-loan associations orchestrated vigorous attacks on public housing initiatives—accusing them of representing unfair government competition with free-market enterprise—and played an important role in organizing local communities to oppose nearby public housing as a tactic to forestall development.[8]

With the recent advent of federal housing vouchers, nonmarket housing in the United States is undergoing a major transformation, as the federal government reduces its role in the development process. Voucher programs provide as much as $9,500 to purchase a new house in Houston or up to $3,500 to purchase and renovate an existing single-family residence, as well as assisting with closing costs and offering courses in buying property and managing credit. The funding takes the form of a lien on the property held by the city during the first five years of ownership; the debt is forgiven if the owners have neither sold nor subleased the property and have maintained good credit. Voucher programs are administered by corporations such as Homes for Houston, a public-private partnership and nonprofit organization established in 1996, which cooperates with other public-private partnerships and nonprofit agencies to identify aid recipients and assist lower-income families in purchasing houses.

The principles that guide voucher programs are based on the belief that homeownership provides lower-income families a greater sense of integration in community and city life than renting does. Individual ownership is thought to create a strong foundation for the redevelopment of neighborhoods that have faced disinvestment; it is intended to reterritorialize these areas by offering residents a stake in their communities. Voucher programs equate landownership with civic representation; they suggest that Cartesian geometry, which describes property and architecture, is capable of effectively providing the taxis, or representational mechanism, of a citizen within the urban economy of the city. As a form of private property, the house is expected to become the essential surface on which an independent and civil life might be inscribed.

The voucher program generally assumes—if not relies on—a racially open or, perhaps, racially unaware housing market, but it arrives in the wake of a history of racial segregation and unequal access to housing. Between 1940 and 1960, public housing for white tenants often sat empty in Houston, even as there was great demand by African American tenants. The architects of *16 Houses* were asked to examine this history of housing policy in Houston, and nationally, and to seek new ways in which design could sustain the pivotal role it has been given in federal policy. Most of them addressed this history in works that deny an easy or convenient closure[9] and display a hesitancy to accept the merits of the program as a whole.

The houses also reflect competing market ideologies, recalling a scenario proposed by Walter Gropius in the 1920s: Gropius advised that German housing be realized using the most advanced, competitive technological and financial practices, but that land acquisition and the eventual sale of the housing be nonspeculative.[10] The architecture of *16 Houses* is derived from competitive financial practices, and also protected from them by the federal funding for the purchase. The cleft is compelling, but not without problems, and most of the houses reveal this conflict in their design. All but one of the participants attempted to meet the market pricing and construction standards of current speculative-housing production— only Interloop Architects disregarded production standards and labor and material constraints. The other fifteen teams were nevertheless reluctant to fully abet the market goals of the voucher program or to condone the shift to market practices.

House as Urban Design

Few types of architecture are as driven by the commodity practices of the market economy as the single-family house. The financing and amortization of housing are extraordinarily sophisticated, but the construction and fabrication are shaped by low-level commodity and labor practices. The result is that the housing market, while sophisticated as a speculative financial field, is underwhelming as a site of architectural or material innovation. Fundamental innovations in the design of housing—or even imaginative modes of housing—are rare if not nonexistent in the United States, and alternative architectural practices that address housing are even rarer (although a prolific press and academia have allowed inventive firms to survive and to offer options outside the constraints of the market).

Unlike the housing design contracts that are awarded in ambitious state-supported competitions in many European countries, architectural commissions in the United States are adjunct to market and speculative development practices. While this arrangement has fostered improved design of products that benefit from large investments in research and development—computers, software, and automobiles, for example—it has done little to improve the quality of housing. The results are evident in every American metropolis and increasingly across the world as other nations emulate the U.S. market economy in housing production. No nation has so fully relinquished the production of housing to market forces as the United States, however, or so fully protected the market as the source, if not the curator, of innovation.

The isolation and interiority that characterized most public housing in the United States were legitimate and pressing reasons to seek alternatives to existing federal programs. Moving public housing in the direction of market housing, however, creates another set of complexities and virtual forms of closure. The voucher system secures the market's right to financial gain in the production of housing, with the understanding that markets will distribute not just form and material, or profits and land, but also domestic and urban space. For architecture, this relationship has often rendered the production of housing a site of political crisis, a negotiation between competing interests that ascribe their legitimacy to the foundations of United States Federalist law. On one hand, the federal government protects the market and what John Locke refers to as "men's different and unequal faculties of acquiring property."[11] On the other, it safeguards the rights to private property and wealth. Housing in the United States must balance these two modes of investment. The housing developer seeks to extract wealth through quick production; that is, the house is used to produce quick profits. The second user, the owner, seeks to secure and localize private wealth and to maintain a feeling of stability and psychological repose in the ownership of the property. The security of these pursuits is, according to Locke, among "the proper tasks of political society,"[12] and cannot but create an essentially divided site.[13]

Since its inception, federal housing policy has attempted to ameliorate these conditions: the poorest members of society have been unable to secure market housing and so the government has essentially redistributed wealth to accommodate needs. Voucher programs mark a significant shift away from New Deal policies and the origins of federal assistance. They seek a new position: they do not provide housing for the poorest members of society but they do operate within the realm of poverty. Houston's FWCRC, for example, serves many who are returning to their childhood neighborhoods as adult homeowners. The house therefore carries a message of weight and importance.

In logic reminiscent of Alexis de Tocqueville, the new programs attempt to provide federal assistance without undermining the goals "of genuinely private property."[14] To do so, vouchers must avoid the semblance of redistribution, or at least overt redistribution; instead, the subsidy they provide, like the development process itself, is strategic, rapid, and intended as an impetus to market practices. While far from a new trend toward Federalist law, the move to vouchers does represent a hybridization of the political left and right—the vouchers legitimize both the need for housing assistance and the role of the market in addressing this need.

As it is positioned within the voucher program, architecture almost necessarily adopts the desire to act on behalf of a lower-income public assumed to be without recourse or representation. It is expected to redistribute space, property, and in essence, wealth—relieving the racial and class-driven crisis endemic to most public housing in the United States—which assumes that private capital can indeed make such provisions for any income group. It isn't clear that architecture can negotiate this double terrain and can actually meet these demands, but that is essentially the challenge offered by the voucher house.

Public House

The role of the single-family house in the postwar city—and the degree to which it is an atomized component of that city—forces it to seek a position that is simultaneously urban and private. *16 Houses* represents the remaking of the house as an agent of retroactive coherence: the house seeks to retroactively reveal the city in revealing its own making. These works of architecture are interested both in their own autonomy (and the security of their inhabitants) and in providing a form of witness to the means of their own apparent inevitability. They are not concerned with an immediate alleviation of market forces or social strife. Each sincerely offers comfort and function but also partially displays its fabrication and labor techniques. As private spaces, they are a form of public art: they train a lens on the material, political, and economic ground of their own making.

Several of the houses—Brunner Pope Architects' Street House, Carlos Jiménez Studio's Peavy, and my own Glass House @ 2 Degrees—are derived from a concept of memory proposed by Henri Bergson. In *Matter and Memory*, Bergson defines a "movement-image" or a "time-image" as an intuited presence[15] situated "between a thing itself" and its representation.[16] These houses offer a "fleeting glimpse"[17] of the city. They are concerned with the potential of the house as an intuiting device,[18] a tool for comprehending urban time and history. In the Jiménez project, architecture is situated between formal fixity as a discrete urban entity and an attempt to forestall the predatory, all-consuming city. The concept of architecture as memory—or time-image in Bergson's lexicon—allows the architects to conceive of a building as a fixed end product of fiscal and political policies, but as relieved of the artificial unity that these policies suppose. Nevertheless, it is difficult to equate the work in *16 Houses*—or the single-family house as an end product that results from federal housing policy—with the forces that produced it. Like other commodities, these houses do not completely reveal their making.

16 Houses exposes architectural practice in the United States—especially the design of lower-income housing—as almost irrelevant in relation to ubiquitous commodity practices. Architects are forced to operate in a crisis mode that fluctuates between market acquiescence and resistance. Despite these constraints, however, they are now being asked to design houses that will serve as agents of citizenship. To do so, they must find ways to literally or symbolically expand the boundaries of the single-family house, transcending the limitations of its relative insignificance within the urban landscape and tapping into the power structures of the larger infrastructure.

Public-Private

Between 1934 and 1974, one of the most significant influences on urban planning in the United States was the design of federally funded housing. Its planning, financing, and, ultimately, architectural form touched on issues ranging from class and race divisions to mental health and social strife. Housing policies have resulted in changes in zoning and building massing, and housing design has been the most fertile testing ground for ideas developed by the prewar European avant-garde. Housing prototypes published by Le Corbusier in 1924—a decade before the establishment of the first federal housing initiatives in the United States—were instrumental in slum clearance.

The National Housing Act of 1934 and the Wagner-Steagall Act of 1937 together allocated $800 million in the form of federal loans to states to develop low-income housing. In New York City, the prospect of $300 million[19] in new federal funds loomed, and the New York City Housing Authority (NYCHA) was formed in anticipation. In the 1940s, these agencies became epicenters of urban development and design. Public housing became what Robert Caro has described as "the great new source of outside money flowing into American cities."[20] Houston, like New York, aggressively sought these funds, which were a major force for urban, political, and social change, even in areas unrelated to housing. The physical form these funds would take was determined by architects and planners; until 1974, when the Nixon administration significantly curtailed funding, housing was the central focus of urban expenditure and policy.

Since its inception, NYCHA, like similar institutions in Houston, Washington, D.C., Chicago, and San Francisco, has variously retreated from and advanced toward its original policies. At the core of this vacillation have been the questions of how to characterize the forces that create poverty and how an empowered entity should formalize its acts of intervention on behalf of a less empowered group. Since 1934, federal housing policy has involved sweeping campaigns to eliminate the conditions of poverty by erasing the sites of poverty, and the government has built enormous urban housing projects that have often

Le Corbusier's Unité d'Habitation in Marseilles (1947–52), *far left,* his Ville Contemporaine (1922), and his Plan Voisin (1925) served as models for early federally funded housing in the United States; since 1996, however, federal voucher programs have promoted the construction of single-family houses, *left,* and low-density, low-rise condominiums

caused more suffering than they alleviated. Edmund Borgia Butler, chairman of NYCHA during its early years, acknowledged the inherent dangers of these programs, insisting that "to justify further public housing, it is necessary to base public housing on something more secure than improvement of the physical condition of the city, by substituting new bricks, mortar, and steel for old . . . Public housing must not be used to regiment the tenants . . . poverty is not the sin of the poor; it is the sin of society."[21] Nevertheless, during his tenure, tens of thousands of tenements were destroyed to "un-slum" the city.[22]

Public housing in the United States currently shelters approximately 1.3 million families,[23] and federal subsidies are still intact, but their point of entry into the development process has moved to strategic points during the development, financing, and eventual private sale. In 1998, the Housing and Urban Development (HUD) budget included funding for a hundred thousand new vouchers—an indication that sixty-four years of design and urban-renewal experiments had given way to a moderated form of free-market development. The public-private partnership—assisted by the voucher and the tax credit—places the house and housing at the interchange of construction, finance, and private life. Under these conditions, design must attempt to create an "economy of visibility"[24] in which the forces that operate in the larger power structure are given some degree of transparency or legibility.

Houston has been at the forefront of these transformations in federal housing policy: as a sprawling city of houses, it offered a pilot site for testing the voucher program's merits and viability. In Houston, the voucher plan was expected to spur the construction and resale of up to twenty-five thousand new and refurbished houses by the year 2000. The program did not meet this goal, primarily because it proved difficult to identify funding recipients. But the neo-privatization of public housing continues unabated. The debates about Houston's voucher program are comparable to those about school vouchers. Early studies indicate that the move to market-rate housing has for some low-income residents proven untenable because of increases in real-estate prices caused by the expanding economy.

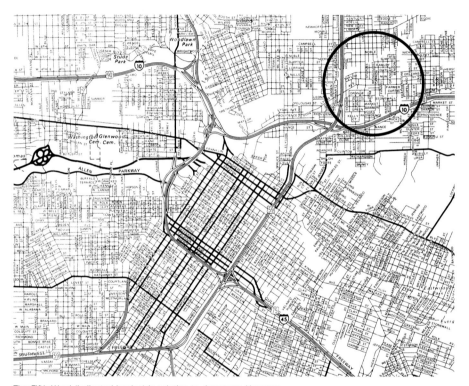

The Fifth Ward (indicated by ring) in relation to downtown Houston

Site

Scattered Sites

During the 1990s, the New York City Housing Authority, like other housing agencies, adopted controversial decentralization policies that met with great resistance, as it was unclear whether they represented a diminished commitment to low-income housing. They also had great support, however, as a legitimate response to the long-simmering crisis of earlier housing initiatives. The City of New York currently provides housing for almost six hundred thousand residents in more than three hundred public housing projects, and it has had fewer social problems (crime, disease, overcrowding) than nearby housing in cities such as Newark, New Jersey.[25] Speculation about the success of New York's projects points to its decentralization policy—the dispersal of housing units (often smaller buildings that do not stand alone) throughout the fabric of the city.[26]

The Fifth Ward Community Redevelopment Corporation provides the same advantage in Houston's Fifth Ward, offering an alternative to typical speculative housing and public-private developments by building affordable single-family houses on sites scattered throughout the community. For *16 Houses*, the FWCRC acted as the client, providing cost parameters and family profiles. The sixteen architects received a breakdown of construction costs and specifications for a typical FWCRC house in Houston and for a building site of fifty by a hundred feet. Houses designed for the exhibition were required to work within the economic constraints of the program; the goal was for each project to meet the buildable criteria and the target sales prices ranging from $36,000 to $82,550.

Numeric Houston: Lost Time

On a given weekday, the aggregate population of Houston drives an average of 53 million miles. At the average speed of commuter traffic, this would amount to a drive time of thirty-five years per day. To drive those thirty-five years every day, Houston residents purchased more than $460 million worth of automobiles in 1996. In the same year, national car sales amounted to $525.9 billion—enough to build 525 Getty Centers.

16 Houses asked the architects to compare the dimensional and numeric value of major infrastructure systems to that of the new federal program that provides financial assistance to lower-income families seeking housing in urban centers. The unfavorable comparison revealed architecture's inability to act as an armature that could compete with the predatory economic forces that shape urban space.

From the 50's to 80's

Plan #650

$ 74,500

✦ Two story

✦ 1,615 sq. ft.

✦ 4 bedrooms, 2.5 bath

✦ 2 car attached garage

This plan features spacious living and dining areas conveniently attached to kitchen/breakfast area. All bedrooms including the master suite and utility room are upstairs. Large walk-in closets in each bedroom. Both baths include a marble vanity, half bath accented with pedestal wash basin. Optional fireplace can be added to living room.

Additional floorplans available soon !

150	One story • 1,007 sq. ft. • 3 bedrooms • 2 bath • 2 car attached garage • extra large family room • breakfast room connects to large kitchen • spacious closets in each bedroom for additional storage	$ 59,990
350	One story • 1,350 sq. ft. • 3 large bedrooms • 2 bath • 2 car attached garage • large family room connected to kitchen and breakfast room for family interaction	$ 68,990
850	Two story • 1,800 sq. ft. • 4 bedrooms • 2.5 bath • 2 car attached garage • formal living and dining rooms • family room attached to kitchen and breakfast area • walk-in closets throughout for extra storage	$ 79,990
950	Two story • 2,000 sq. ft. • 4 bedrooms • 2.5 bath • 2 car attached garage • formal living and dining rooms • family room attached to kitchen and breakfast area • walk-in closets throughout for extra storage	$ 83,990

Developer advertisement for a voucher house

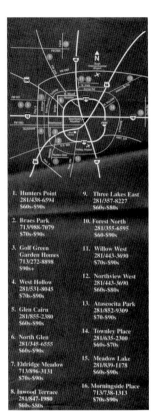

1. **Hunters Point** 281/438-6594 $60s-$90s
2. **Braes Park** 713/988-7079 $70s-$90s
3. **Golf Green Garden Homes** 713/272-8898 $90s+
4. **West Hollow** 281/531-8045 $70s-$90s
5. **Glen Cairn** 281/855-2380 $60s-$90s
6. **North Glen** 281/345-6555 $60s-$90s
7. **Eldridge Meadow** 713/896-3131 $70s-$90s
8. **Inwood Terrace** 281/847-1980 $60s-$80s
9. **Three Lakes East** 281/357-8227 $60s-$80s
10. **Forest North** 281/355-6595 $60-$90s
11. **Willow West** 281/443-3690 $70s-$90s
12. **Northview West** 281/443-3690 $60s-$80s
13. **Atascocita Park** 281/852-9309 $70-$90s
14. **Townley Place** 281/635-2300 $60s-$70s
15. **Meadow Lake** 281/839-1178 $60s-$90s
16. **Morningside Place** 713/738-1313 $70s-$90s

Market-rate developments in Houston scattered throughout the city

An FWCRC house and a senior-citizen housing complex (developed with the Pleasant Hills Baptist Church) in the Fifth Ward

DO YOU QUALIFY?

HOMEBUYER EDUCATION REGISTRATION FORM

Your gross income, along with that of family members living in your home, may not exceed the amounts listed below:

HOUSEHOLD SIZE	MAXIMUM INCOME
1 PERSON	$25,750
2 PERSONS	$29,450
3 PERSONS	$33,100
4 PERSONS	$36,800
5 PERSONS	$39,750
6 PERSONS	$42,700
7 PERSONS	$45,650
8 PERSONS	$48,550

PERSONAL INFORMATION

NAME OF APPLICANT: NAME OF CO-APPLICANT:

SOCIAL SECURITY NUMBER: SOCIAL SECURITY NUMBER:

RESIDENT ADDRESS: CITY, STATE, ZIP:

DO YOU PREFER TO TAKE THE CLASS DURING: □ TUE/THURS EVENINGS □ SAT ALL DAY □ SAT MORNING /AFTERNOON

HOW DID YOU HEAR OF OUR COUNSELING PROGRAM? □ FRIEND □ RADIO/TV □ BANK □ REALTY □ NEWSPAPER □ CITY □ OTHER (specify)

HOME PHONE: WORK PHONE:

NUMBER OF PEOPLE IN HOUSEHOLD: GROSS ANNUAL INCOME:

In order to qualify for any of the City of Houston and Harris County Housing Assistance Programs, you must purchase your home in the City and County eligible areas and eligible crossertain restrictions apply. Please call our office at 713-644-8488 to verify eligibility. In general your credit performance and the credit performance of any Co-Applicant must be good. TO REGISTER FOR CLASSES PLEASE COMPLETE REGISTRATION FORM AND SEND MONEY ORDER IN THE AMOUNT OF $25.00 TO:

HOUSING OPPORTUNITIES OF HOUSTON, INC.
2900 WOODRIDGE, SUITE 300
HOUSTON, TEXAS 77087
No Personal Checks Accepted for Registration

FOR OFFICE USE ONLY		
Applicant is ___% of median income	Class For □ Week Day □ WeekEnd	Registration Fee Rec'd □ Yes □ No
Applicant class Schedule is ___	City HAP □ County HAP □ SCAN □	□ Money order □ Check □ Cash
Applicant Class is □ English □ Spanish	Over Income Guidelines □ Yes □ No	To Return □ To Call □

ALL LOANS ARE SUBJECT TO LENDER APPROVAL

Determining eligibility for assistance: home-buyer education registration form

---

METROBANK
NATIONAL ASSOCIATION

MORTGAGE DIVISION

OFFERS UP TO

$9,500.00*

TO PURCHASE A HOME

Assistance in Financing and Home Buyer Counseling

Income to $48,550 (depending on family size)

OK for New Homes or Existing Homes*

CALL: 713 - 414-3558
OR
713 - 924-4519

* Amount of assistance available is based on income, family size and the purchase of a new home or previously occupied home. Ask our mortgage representatives for these guidelines.

MetroBank advertisement for voucher assistance

HOUSTON HOUSING PARTNERSHIP (HHP)
HOUSING ASSISTANCE PROGRAM (HAP)

Amount of Assistance:	Between $1,000 to $3,500
	0% interest, 5 year term, forgiven 20% per year if property remains owner occupied and mortgage is paid as agreed
Assistance to be used:	up to 2% towards downpayment, closing costs and/or prepaids
Borrower Eligibility:	Income not to exceed 80% of area median; must attend 5 hours (2 sessions) of Home Buyer Counseling at Housing Opportunities of Houston
Property Eligibility:	New or existing Within city limits of Houston Must meet HUD Housing Quality Standards including Lead-Based paint Single family, townhouse, condominium, manufactured housing Maximum sales price $96,250
Financing:	Conventional, FHA, VA or lender portfolio

Income limits:

Family Size	Income	Family Size	Income
1	$25,750	5	$39,750
2	$29,450	6	$42,700
3	$33,100	7	$45,650
4	$36,800	8	$48,550

Call Housing Opportunities of Houston
to set up Home Buyer Counseling
644-8488

Homes for Houston application form

PARTICIPANTS COMMITMENTS

- Your home will be a HACH rehabilitated residence which meets FHA and Federal Housing Quality Standards.

- You are required to receive six hours of home buyer training.

- You must live in the home as your permanent residence for a 10 year Period.

- You will have to qualify for a loan with a mortgage lender.

- You must have enough cash savings for closing costs and down payment, which can be as low as $1,000. or around 4% of the sales price.

- You must have acceptable credit to meet the standards of the mortgage lender financing the home.

- Your monthly payments will be between $300 and $600 depending on the price of the home. Income to qualify for the program can be as low as $1,000. per month, depending on the price of the home and the amount of your outstanding bills.

- You may have a non-resident to cosign for the purchase of the home.

Housing Authority of the City of Houston leaflet

Ownership, Equity, Representation, and Design

The voucher program has created an opportunity for more people to purchase their own houses. It is not clear, however, whether homeownership actually abets representation or even economic empowerment, although it does create a sense of inclusion and stability. To explore this question, I compiled data in design-research studios that I taught at Rice and Columbia Universities between 1996 and 2001. These studios addressed the issue of housing as it relates to the economic processes of commercial development. The interests that guided the research were not aesthetic, or even initially architectural; our goal was to ascertain the constituent value of a single-family house in Houston's economy. (Even though it is the fourth largest city in the United States, Houston is almost exclusively a city of single-family houses.) The following survey of that data addresses the value of homeownership within the context of urban finance.

What is the scope of the voucher program in relation to other Houston expenditures? The voucher program will provide housing assistance to twenty-five thousand families. The total value of the program depends on the ratio of new to existing houses purchased within its guidelines. The program could offer as much as $225 million in assistance or as little as $75 million.[27] When these numbers are compared with expenditures by the Texas Department of Transportation in Houston, some startling insights surface. For example, the Texas DOT[28] currently administers almost $1.4 billion in Houston-area highway construction contracts. During 1996 alone, road construction costs in Houston reached $457 million, and maintenance of existing roadways, $57 million. In comparison, the voucher program is relatively small. Should it be bigger? Could it be bigger? The recent construction of one segment of freeway in Houston cost approximately $22 million a mile; at this rate, three and a half miles of freeway could fund the entire voucher program at its low estimate (in fact, the total cost of the eight-mile freeway in question was more than $182 million).[29] Houston has approximately eighty-seven hundred miles of freeway; the actual distance and cost are almost impossible to calculate.

Is it possible to design a house in Houston that would accrue equity at an accelerated rate? The average single-family house in Houston is sold approximately every nine years. At that point, assuming an initial mortgage of $50,000, the homeowner would have amassed $6,589 in equity, having made mortgage payments totaling $38,232, or approximately $354 per month.[30] As these calculations demonstrate, ownership through the voucher program provides little more than personal satisfaction and self-esteem. These numbers do not account for the federal income tax deductions that accompany a mortgage, nor do they include added monthly costs such as insurance, property tax, school taxes, or utility fees. Ownership in this average scenario clearly does not provide the economic empowerment and representation it is assumed to, nor is it necessarily a better economic situation than renting. Is there a way that architectural design could facilitate a faster accrual of equity? For example: full equity in a $25,000 automobile could be accrued in five years at a monthly expense of $502.34.[31] In Houston, it may be conceivable to build a $25,000, three-bedroom house. If this house offered even modest innovation in energy efficiency, it could be possible to allocate savings in monthly utilities expenditures to the higher mortgage payments that would come with a short-term loan. Equity could be amassed at a tremendously accelerated rate. It may be possible to design a house in which full equity is accrued in five years, even within the cost guidelines of the voucher program. Innovation in energy use alone could make a dramatic difference in how affordable these houses are; innovation in labor processes involved in construction could also affect the affordability and quality of the houses.

How does the market develop houses in Houston? The voucher program assumes that the market can and will produce houses more efficiently than federal or city housing agencies. Developer houses in Houston are routinely offered for sale at prices as low as $55,000, and are within the reach of many families who might otherwise rely on the voucher program. Innovation, however, in simple functionality, design, and quality of materials is nonexistent. The voucher program hopes to rely on the free market to provide a decent level of housing. Will it? Does the building industry have the will to innovate? Clearly, architects have had little success in infiltrating the machinations of housing development. The term "housing starts," which is often used to describe the health of the economy, almost invariably refers to a kind of construction that implies the demise of architecture as we have valued it.

Consider the following case study of Sable Ridge. (This information was culled from private interviews with the developer; "Sable Ridge" is a pseudonym.) A Houston subdivision of 347 boxlike houses, Sable Ridge was built in the late 1980s at a total cost of $16 million. It is situated outside the Houston Beltway, or Loop, in an area currently growing in population at a rate of more than 10 percent per annum. Compaq Computers, whose headquarters are in this area, accounts for much of this growth. The cost of construction for housing built at Sable Ridge was thirty-three dollars per square foot.[32] Architectural fees for this project of more than five-hundred thousand square feet were $4,550, or almost 0.028 percent of the total construction costs. The entire subdivision could have been constructed on an average Houston city block (there are countless empty downtown blocks) at a height of five stories, but architectural fees for a single building of that size would have amounted to more than $1.4 million[33]—therefore, the developers of Sable Ridge made a profit of nearly $2 million.

Building materials for a single house at Sable Ridge have a relative value of approximately ten thousand dollars per house if bought on a per-house basis at a retail hardware store. The rest of the costs are accounted for by labor, advertising, and profit. The market provides no incentive to build in the city center or to use architectural services. It does not provide the components or the innovation that could make the voucher program a success in terms of providing meaningful civic representation. It will build houses and it will assert that the geometric dimensions of the box, the plot of land, and the street are all capable of providing economic representation, but the simple fact remains that they only provide a psychological boost. While architects may offer formal solutions that mime topology, architecture's critical role in the city will find its resonance in the infiltration and rearrangement of the clandestine and essentially predatory forms of finance and development.

The guidelines set by the Houston voucher program are restrictive but not without potential or aesthetic challenge. A family of four must earn less than $36,800 to qualify for assistance. Proposed designs for new and renovated houses built within the limits of the market could make a real and significant contribution not only to this strata of our population but to our concept of the contemporary city as a whole. The voucher houses could be some of the best works of architecture of our time.

Redistribution

Adding Equity

The voucher plan adds equity to a housing purchase by adding financial value at the front end of the sale. It gives the buyer a boost and a head start in the process of ownership, and is a shield against accrued interest. Equity, however, is dramatically affected by the way a building is produced long before it is purchased. The standard mass-produced American house, as a product of building trades such as drywalling and framing, accrues value—surplus—for the developer based on efficient division of labor and the replication of basic building forms. Most of the houses proposed here address this problem and, in some cases, embrace these conditions, expediting the division of labor or proposing new means of labor altogether. The Klip House by Interloop Architects and the Variable House by Chuihua Judy Chung and Sze Tsung Leong both articulate the division of building components and fabrication techniques.

The *16 Houses* call for proposals asked each team to address the issue of fabrication in light of theories of labor and production: in each case, the referenced texts were familiar to the architects in relation to architectural and urban theory, but not in relation to the political and cultural aspects of poverty found in U.S. housing projects. Texts by Adam Smith[34] and Moishe Postone[35] were given as touchstones and, in effect, forced a reconciliation of Marxist labor themes, which are frequently part of the critical discourse of American and European modernism, with American practices of housing production and racial segregation. The architects invited to participate in *16 Houses* had all shown an engagement with the political histories of capitalism and architecture—with architecture as a means of labor and the production of wealth—and with themes of alienation, but had not designed public hous-

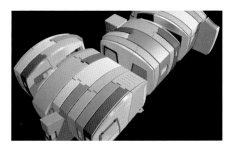

Klip House by Mark Wamble and Dawn Finley
(Interloop Architects)

Variable House by Chuihua Judy Chung and
Sze Tsung Leong

ing. They brought their experience to bear on developing new modes of housing in a milieu that encouraged them to cover new intellectual and pragmatic ground.

In works such as the Klip House and the Variable House, the architects propose a domestic space and a private realm that embrace the market in an effort to preempt the market's hegemony; the architecture attempts to objectify the market before the market can objectify it. The architects of the Klip House provide a set of protocols that suggest that maintenance could be coupled with upgrading and exchange. They compare the house and its component parts to commodities such as cars and televisions, which can be traded in, and suggest that the Klip system could respond similarly to a client's changing needs. The architects of the Variable House also propose that the house be standardized for production efficiency, so that it can be disassembled and changed as new needs arise.

Stanley Saitowitz's project, One of Sixteen Houses, also embraces building commodity processes, but instead of suggesting that materials or processes be upgraded, it makes use of lower-level construction techniques. Saitowitz's house is composed of conventional wood framing and a concrete slab, but he writes in the gallery text that it "weaves and folds inside and out, over and under" itself. Calling the house a "double terrain," he likens it to a tube "unwinding on itself, and looking at itself through itself from itself." An off-the-shelf assembly, its cubic geometry recalls the topology of a Möbius strip, tempered by standard construction techniques.

In the Feedback House, Blair Satterfield and Marc Swackhamer attempt to eliminate the fit and finish of construction and to loosen joints and seams between elements. By reducing the intricacy of detailing, they are able to treat walls economically as continuous planes; the smooth surfaces form backdrops for everyday objects. The architects allow the house to exist as an object in its own right by letting it reveal its own making. Satterfield and Swackhamer write in the gallery text that this revelation of the construction process—seeing the house as an assemblage of discrete parts—allows one to imagine the labor that went into the structure. The house is described as a "feedback" loop, "a device that registers and records" its own presence.

StudioWorks's house is also constructed with what the architects refer to as the "most standard and economical existing-found building methods." Relying on "raw bulk materials,"

One of Sixteen Houses by Stanley Saitowitz

Cosmos of Houses by StudioWorks

it is one of several houses that use Hardiplank and Hardipanel, MDF, concrete block, and structural plastic wall panels such as General Electric Thermoclear. StudioWorks writes a kind of scripted litany of building techniques: "Standard parts, etc., are accessorized and supplemented through carefully chosen accouterments and additives. The accouterments and additives take the form of things like a 96¢ cast-plastic lamp receptacle, . . . a 75¢ cast-aluminum door handle, paint, concrete stain, etc."

StudioWorks, Saitowitz, Interloop, and Chung/Leong—indeed most of the architects—fabricate the private house from a self-reflexive schema of standard construction. The Game House by TAFT Architects and Nonya Grenader was inspired by Charles and Ray Eames's Little Expandable House toy of 1959. TAFT has practiced in Houston for more than twenty-five years, and the gaming strategy here is a new version of earlier work that used color-coded systems and modular components.

Only the Klip House, however, suggests a higher level of production both materially and through labor processes. The architects' fundamental goal was to create a housing type that could take advantage of the high-end production techniques of companies such as Microsoft, Sony, and General Electric—the very multinational corporations that are understood to have fractured the territorial clarity of the historic city. Klip housing components are manufactured by major corporations with access to research and development capital, but none of these entities dominates the final form. Also, rather than atomizing the federal funding allocated to voucher programs, the architects of the Klip House suggest pooling that money to create a research-and-development fund that would allow a higher level of manufacture.

The labor processes of market-rate housing present an opportunity for design innovations that synthesize dimensions not usually studied by designers. Most of the teams therefore focused on the construction process, examining both on-site and off-site potentials for innovation. Houses currently built within the developer market and the voucher program, however, do not avail themselves of the kind of innovations proposed by Interloop, or even the more imminently feasible techniques proposed by Chung/Leong, Satterfield/Swackhamer, Keith Krumwiede, and TAFT/Grenader. Moreover, the production of houses in the market economy as it stands is a surplus mechanism; dividing labor into discrete trades provides a return on investment that is exponential, yet the end product—the house—should be able

Game House by TAFT Architects and Nonya Grenader

Feedback House by Blair Satterfield and Marc Swackhamer

to reveal the accrued labor of its workers. The house should allow you to intuit its making and the dimensional attributes of its economy. In doing so, it could become a time-image of its own making—the house in its transparency could be lived in. At times the transparency would reveal internal life, and at other times it would reveal the city.

Redistributing Wealth: Federalist Law, Federal House

Federalist era law has historically been the conservative benchmark that challenged overt redistribution of monies or property to compensate for free-market inadequacies in dealing with poverty. On the cusp of the nineteenth century, Federalist law countered attempts at a legislated redistribution of monolithic forms of wealth, even as theorists recognized that free-market rights to private property had the dangerous potential to damage equality by pooling wealth. In a society that protected property rights and the potentially exploitive monetary gain they portend, Federalist law also protected the individual right to gains made in a free market, even if those gains often seemed intolerable in light of losses suffered by the apparently less industrious.[36]

The advent of the voucher programs signifies that the federal government is adopting an increasingly conservative view of housing development. Architects who routinely consider theirs to be an aesthetic practice based in the virtuous search for civic life find themselves at odds with twentieth-century mercantile practices, from highly standardized Taylorist work practices to amortized return on investments. One could argue that the practice of architecture in the United States is increasingly one of creating private property; the public realm is an afterthought rather than the result of an agenda. Federal housing projects have come to symbolize the absolute power that was not only wielded over a group of people, but that essentially revealed their poverty in its collectivity by giving it architectural form. The market is now expected to fix what sixty years of housing policy has created. Fundamental principles imbedded in United States political theory and law, however, virtually assure that whatever form the new housing takes, it will be quite literally a conservative emblem of the market—and, of course, redistributed housing does not at all guarantee redistributed wealth.

Into the Market

Sometime around 1929, the percentage of the United States gross national product that could be attributed to steel production reached its peak. The quantity of steel produced continued to increase, and its per capita usage in the United States continued to climb until the 1970s, but it was no longer the benchmark industry for the U.S. economy. In the late 1970s, the production of plastic surpassed that of steel.

Architecture conceived around the new steel and glass technologies at the turn of the century was staged in a manufacturing economy that, according Moishe Postone, took advantage of modern labor processes, yet allowed workers to work "in" and "for the city"[37]—their relationship with production made them feel connected to their products. In an environment that divided labor and relied on segregate worker tasks, a quasi-territorial relationship with space, work, city, and family was still possible. In the early twentieth century, manufacturing could ideally produce "objects that functioned as carriers of a common spirit," and "that spirit" could constitute "economic prosperity."[38]

If steel was the vanguard product of the new factory and was responsible for the accrual of surplus value through segregated factory labor, glass was the counterpart call to transparency, equality, openness, and commonly held collective space. Using glass today in a low-income house in Houston, however, obviously doesn't achieve these ideals—the degree to which factory-produced housing elements such as sliding glass doors offer workers a sense of their common accomplishment or represent a synthesis of art and technology is presumably almost nil. In fact, in his essay "Chain of Glass," Massimo Cacciari depicts glass, or transparency, as having become a predatory tool that "desecrates" private experience.[39] Cacciari's reading of Mies van der Rohe's work is of a glass house in which there is no need for an interior because there is "nothing left to collect."[40]

The myriad products found in contemporary houses are advanced in terms of chemical properties, production techniques, and distribution systems. Unlike the products it houses, however, the architecture is often cloaked in nostalgic garb that disguises its technological advances, suggesting that our private and territorial lives are still intact. The *16 Houses* projects, on the other hand, openly question the idea of private space: Interloop, for example, surrounds the occupants of its house with corporate products, as if to remind them that there is no longer any escape from corporate branding. How can the private experiences of life be promoted within the means of a lower- (or even moderate-) income house? Can the most banal building elements, such as aluminum, plastic, or resin flooring, still be innovative? The ordinary things that make up our households—a water glass, a beaker, a pressurized canister, a plastic pillbox—should convince us that we continue to be extraordinarily innovative in producing common goods, though we rarely allow them to influence our architecture as we did in the early part of the last century.

Keith Krumwiede's house, the Domestic Topographic Package, addresses affordability through economies of scale. In its primary volume, this house uses a structural steel frame manufactured off-site by a Houston-area shipbuilding factory. Houston clay soils usually demand extensive grade beams and foundations, but the rigidity of this frame allows for a columnar foundation and greatly reduced foundation costs. Krumwiede's house incorporates short-run prefabrication techniques as well, which, according to the architect, allow "a flexible domestic environment that exceeds the systemization of its construction." The project was presented with a series of short stories by Carol Treadwell, describing the intimate life of the house's occupants in spatial terms. According to Krumwiede's gallery text, "The DTP breaks the conventional single-family house open and pulls it up and across three levels, constructing a fluid domestic topography at the scale of the site. Each layer of the house exploits its unique position and is linked to the others through various openings and material continuities (or slipped surfaces) that integrate the house across its section, generating a variably dense and expansive interior that capitalizes on the interconnectedness of different phases of family life."

Krumwiede's house is typical of many works included here in that it attempts to create a complementary relationship between the intimacy of private life and the surfaces of mass production. It offers an objectification of the house and its construction techniques, as well as objectifying its occupants. Like Glass House @ 2 Degrees, it vacillates between privacy and exposure.

The demands placed on the voucher house led many of the architects to use transparency not as a mode of nihilism, but as a form of self-objectification. Public housing has historically objectified its inhabitants: here the objectification is turned inside out. Rather than living in what Michel Foucault has called the "shade" of power, many of these works quite literally find domestic space in a liberal acceptance of the visibility Foucault claims power requires of its subject.[41] In these houses, the means of construction and finance are revealed, resulting in places of unanticipated respite—the houses may be mass-produced, but they are surprisingly unthreatening because they don't try to camouflage it. Nor do they try to disguise their attempt to satisfy two constituencies with often conflicting needs, the developer and the buyer.

Several of the architects challenged the budget parameters, questioning how the valuation of the houses was determined. The house designed by Lars Lerup and Thumb was accompanied by a text that suggested that the idea of building a low-cost house was troubling in a country that controls an inordinate share of the world's wealth. Lerup and Thumb designed a house whose primary volume was a prefabricated metal shed, commonly used in Houston for garages and warehouses; ironically, it was one of the lowest-cost proposals. Facades that featured text written by Sanford Kwinter and designed by Bruce Mau were not visible in the final proposal, but are presented in this book. The text was inspired by James Joyce and was written in a meter that depicted a perpetual, self-referential transformation intended to capture the spirit of what the architects of *16 Houses* felt was an essential crisis in American housing production: Kwinter's text attempts to reproduce the infinitely complex and autonomous numeric transformations in financial and production systems, as well

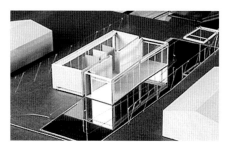

Glass House @ 2 Degrees by Michael Bell

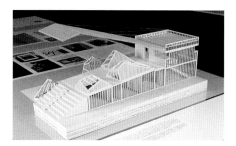

Street House by Brunner Pope Architects

as the way that the housing developments themselves are replicated ad infinitum with only the slightest formal changes.

From the outset, *16 Houses'* mandate was to address the urgent needs of Fifth Ward residents, who were mistrustful of the new federal voucher programs because of the complex inequities that have historically characterized public housing in the United States. The houses are not idealized works; the architects set aside any attempt to create virtuoso formal works in order to design houses that could be built within the constraints of the voucher program. At the same time, an almost universal ambivalence about accepting these constraints—and thereby endorsing the premise of the voucher program—expressed itself in all of the houses. In one way or another, each attempts to bridge the gap between residents' immediate needs and that which would be theoretically possible if one could access other forms of wealth or power.

Lindy Roy addresses this conundrum in a house derived from southern typologies, which expresses its desire to tap into the financial power of the urban system with a basinlike pitched roof that reaches up to catch the light of the street lamp—literally attempting to draw energy from the infrastructure. On a more pragmatic level, her house is also a self-cooling structure that attempts to reduce utility costs.

While houses such as the Klip House, the Variable House, and the Feedback House suggest a major, if not total, renovation of housing production systems, most of the houses depict the struggle between actual and ideal without attempting to alter existing building and financial systems. Walter Hood's gardens, designed with input from Thumb, are emblematic of his work in Oakland, California, which combines grassroots redevelopment strategies with improvisation and collage. Like his public gardens in Oakland, Hood's work in *16 Houses* is functional yet complex enough to encourage dialogue about what many consider the current political crisis in housing.

Domestic Architecture and Private Art

Economics and Art

In the fall of 1959, John Kenneth Galbraith accepted an invitation from the Museum of Modern Art to deliver a lecture on economics and art. He prefaced his lecture with the comment that his interest in art and architecture had never produced a clear certainty as to what constituted the "good" and the "less good," but that he was persuaded that "improving economic well-being requires an increasingly close relationship between the artist and economic life," and that alienation between the two would produce a "disappointing and even frustrating banality."

As federal housing policy now moves toward being shaped by market forces, Galbraith's logic is being tested in new circumstances. His lecture touched on the role of the architect, whose goals he portrayed as being at odds with an economically motivated society unconcerned with aesthetics. Galbraith reminded his audience that after World War II, in reaction to the constraints of war and the wartime controls enforced by a strong central administration, planning—especially aesthetic planning—had become an "evil word" and was considered a legislated imposition. The idea of uncontrolled and economically driven development was not only thought to be "justified" in such a context, it was also seen as morally good. Federal housing policy is now attempting to move closer to this essentially postwar sentiment: the city is expected to grow within the market and the market to provide for essential human needs. Art, in other words, should stay out of the way, and architects should respond to the demands of a free market.

To illustrate his thesis, Galbraith showed an image of a stretch of real estate along the Charles River in Cambridge, which included a building by Eero Saarinen. What Galbraith would have considered the obvious beauty of Saarinen's building was challenged by the proximity of new commercial structures—gas stations, shops, warehouses—whose design and form were determined by economic constraints. These structures may have undermined the value of Saarinen's building, but for Galbraith they contributed to a scenario that might create an entirely new value. As the "natural" result of a system that not only seeks efficiency, but also sees "freedom" in efficiency, these structures, Galbraith insisted, had unquestionable merit.

The projects designed for *16 Houses* faced a similar situation. Housing developments, as they are administered in voucher programs, have been reduced to highly efficient artifacts of mass production—commodities. Derived from what Galbraith describes as the "classical trinity of productive forces, land, labor, and capital," *16 Houses* sought what Galbraith has called a fourth factor, one that acts at an entrepreneurial level to organize or manage the proportional relation of the other three factors. For *16 Houses,* that fourth factor was design, particularly since the voucher program has moved federal housing initiatives into the realm of the market and almost fully eliminated the role of design as it is normally valued and sustained in the architectural profession.

16 Houses was guided, in part, by Galbraith's ideas and the desire to find architectural potential amid the mechanisms of commerce, finance, and labor in housing production. The designers—specifically, StudioWorks, Interloop, Chung/Leong, Saitowitz, Jiménez, and Satterfield/Swackhamer—produced works that melded the spatial qualities of architecture with the urban dimensions of production. The Variable House by Chung/Leong emphasizes speed through transformation, and Interloop suggests accelerating the commodity process, just as design in Galbraith's logic operates as a market factor dominated by speed. Glass House @ 2 Degrees is similarly preoccupied with speed and ease of construction, while attempting to find dimensional depth in transparency. Providing a counter to these approaches, Jiménez writes in the gallery text that his house aspires "to prolong the life span, potential, and quality of the house beyond its already implacable economic limits."

Monumental House

After the Second World War, at the outset of a period of tremendous economic growth in the United States, Louis Kahn, who had spent the first twenty-seven years of his career on housing, began to design institutional buildings that sought a monumental presence. Kahn's postwar projects, which integrate the ideals of the collective in singular public works, are the result of a complex algebraic approach with dimensional and scalar qualities that goes beyond the additive and fundamentally stable geometries in his earlier works. In the Yale University Art Gallery (1951), the City Tower (1952–57) done with Anne Tyng, and the Richards Medical Research Building (1957–65), he uses a structural geometry that grows in both an additive and exponential taxis.

The publication of Kahn's essay "Monumentality" in 1944 marks the beginning of this movement away from the goals of *existence minimum* and the low-cost housing projects of his early career and toward institutional projects with symbolic and spiritual value. That essay, with its speculation about the need for monumental modern architecture, appeared a year after Sigfried Giedion, José Luis Sert, and Fernand Léger met in New York to discuss directing modernism's energies away from the "realm of domestic architecture and private art" in favor of institutional works that could satisfy "the eternal demand of the people for translation of their collective force into symbols."[42]

In 1944, while the U.S. government was establishing itself as the world's preeminent economic and political force, Kahn was steadfastly adhering to a career-long search for the civil and spiritual potentials of architecture. After 1944, during the international effort to enact the Bretton Woods Treaty, he began to formulate an architecture that might sustain the principals of democracy and individualism in the emerging global economy. The scale of America's surplus was accelerating exponentially, and Kahn renewed his concept of architecture to compensate. After 1951, he initiated an investigation of architecture that could embody both the classical inscription of the individual and the machinic dimensions—the exponential growth—of a new national and world economy that was unparalleled in its omnipotence.

Today, more than fifty years later, the production of housing is still defined by the parameters set in motion at the close of World War II. The works presented in *16 Houses* are houses for the postwar city, which to an unprecedented degree relinquished the production of individual housing in favor of the market-produced house. *16 Houses* addresses concerns present in both stages of Kahn's career. The architects were asked to ply their technical expertise in the realm of political policy in a way that defines the house as a monument and a new tool of political power. Despite their modest size and often rudimentary fabrication techniques, however, these houses attempt to respond to the atomization of the postwar city without recourse to the empowerment of institutional authority. They serve needs that are both domestic and institutional—without a coherent urbanism, they must operate in simultaneous realms.

The generation of work shown in *16 Houses* is materially based in the postwar housing efforts that reflected the emergent economy: the Case Study houses built in Los Angeles—and more recent works by Morphosis, Eric Owen Moss, Frank Israel, and Frank Gehry—represent their technical and domestic heritage. StudioWorks, Lindy Roy, TAFT/Grenader, Morris Gutierrez, and Natalye Appel are also colleagues in material detailing, type, and vernacular. Similarly, projects such as Glass House @ 2 Degrees, Klip House, Variable House, Street House, and the Peavy were influenced by the Case Study houses in efficiency of production, but were also influenced by Aldo Rossi's dialectics and work on negative philosophy. Strains of Theodor Adorno's work are also present, as these houses approach critical practices based in negation. To quote Adorno, "Freedom can be defined in negation only. Corresponding to the concrete form of a specific unfreedom."[43] Infused with varying degrees of flexibility and potential transformation, these works do not form a unified body, but they suggest a theoretical proximity to the critical works of Peter Eisenman and, in particular, the writings of Manfredo Tafuri. Here one finds a conflation of existentialism and moderated efficiency: these works are reluctantly seeking to engage the market, but are also trying to define the terms of that engagement.

The Hopscotch Trot house by David Brown falls somewhere between the two extremes. Brown's work suggests a role for improvisation in accepting limitations and finding opportunities within them. It reflects his soon-to-be-published research on jazz and the architecture of Le Corbusier, which reveals influences that have been left unmined in modern architectural history. Brown's house was also influenced by the *Pamphlet Architecture* publication by Steven Holl on rural housing types.

Natalye Appel's houses combine historic typology with local narrative. Scattered throughout the Fifth Ward, each has a unique occupant and story of ownership. Appel has been recognized for her inventive work in Houston in overcoming the challenges of tight budgets and low-cost materials. She makes use of locally manufactured products, such as aluminum windows, stuccos, and plasters, to create a domestic surface derived from the local economy. Similarly, William Williams and Archie Pizzini attempted to spend the federal money in a way that supported the community and spurred capital improvements to local factories and merchants. The market-rate house is among the most economically nonterritorial commodities produced in the United States, and the works in *16 Houses* all attempted to address the degree to which the house is able to provide not only a context for private life but also a financial means for creating local surplus.

I Am Disappeared

"Mobility makes people more tolerant of inequality," said a member of the Brookings Institution in a 1999 interview. "We may tolerate even more inequality if it comes with the perception of even more mobility." Architecture and the freedoms it promises have always attempted to evade the real and imagined oppressions of capital, but increasingly it is clear that capital itself has acquired characteristics of extreme mobility, transformation, and immanent mutability. If speed is the locus of authority at the end of this century, form had better get faster.

It's impossible to count the number of slow failures that have provided architecture immense success. Or the number of times that staging a disappearing act has been a sublimely gratifying tactic for architects. But when the sign of the times is an increasingly pronounced class structure exacerbated by conservative readings of political principle that could not have anticipated the tyranny of speed in the past century, one must ask what recourse is available. It's hard not to believe that a loss of form and negative philosophy have been a fruitful kind of camouflage for a generation of influential architects who hoped to thwart the authority of form, but when power is clandestine and mobile, one wonders if we are playing hide-and-seek and both of the parties are hiding. The ambitions are immense: architecture often promises results beyond its ethical or practical province. It does so in hopes of providing transparency to a society that has at times been opaque—a society that has almost predetermined our memories. The real memories have inexorably disappeared; in a tragicomedy of the architectural sublime, we have long settled for memories of freedom. For Michel Foucault, freedom was never capable of being described as a form but only as a practice,[44] yet the practice of form-making in America is one that rarely includes the participant lives of mobile citizens.

In the Fifth Ward, we would like to remember the things that didn't happen and could have—the events that were missed. Here, architecture reaches beyond the stillness of the moment, yet also necessarily finds movement in that stillness. The Klip House, the Glass House @ 2 Degrees, the Variable House, and the Satterfield/Swackhamer and Brunner Pope houses—indeed most of the works—are simultaneously on the cusp of negation and smoothness. The project by Brunner Pope Architects, in particular, walks this line: constructed of normative two-by-fours and plaster, it conforms to the standard level of construction in Houston. Its massing and entry sequence, however, bring the sidewalk and street up and over the bedrooms, creating a continuous surface between private and public spaces. The house fuses the natural vegetation and the low-grade chain-link fence; again, the role of economy prevails, but so too do the ubiquitous natural systems of Houston. The house is mute in its choice of materials, but startling in the way it suggests they be combined. Public and private life meet at a crucible—the now-recessive front door and elongated entry. There is still a reason to refrain from expression, to renounce the collecting that characterizes private life, but there is little need to accept a future defined by the technical, labor, and material relations of market-rate housing in the United States. These works are ultimately a conflation of means—some derived from early modern architecture, others from vernacular, and others still from contemporary building trades. The houses are in many ways acting as useful monuments: each is functional, but each in its inchoate manifestation signifies a future that is still a promise.

During the 1990s, Houston gained almost six hundred thousand new residents, yet it had no comprehensive housing policy. By 1999, estimates of stock ownership in the United States placed 88.4 percent of publicly traded stock in the hands of just 10 percent of the population, a figure that had risen from a 1983 base of 68.2 percent; the wealthiest 1 percent owned 51.4 percent of all stock. To an unprecedented degree, our built environment is now produced by this same market—but can the market produce architecture? And for whom is the market most effective? For a profession that judges its success by the emblematic visibility and agency of built form, form has become nothing less than a generation-long source of ambivalence and crisis. We need form and we resist it as it is consistently revealed to be determined by factors beyond our control.

16 Houses is a small event that has grown into a large community effort. The projects are inventive and powerful, but the collaboration is the most significant aspect. As an ongoing project, its challenge is to create new events and additional collaborations. *16 Houses* sought new building types, new construction techniques, and new programming to add to the history of housing types already in place. In doing so, it tried to enrich the voucher program's goal of civic inclusion by using design as an entrepreneurial element that calibrates the disparate forces in the contemporary city.

The event eclipses the forms. In the words of Michel Foucault, "Liberty is a practice; it does not and cannot take a form . . . the exercise of freedom is however not indifferent to spatial distribution . . . it can only function when there is a certain convergence; in the case of divergence or distortion, it immediately becomes the opposite of what was intended."[45]

Postscript

Far Rockaway: The Past and the Future Converge

In 2001, the New York Department of Housing, Preservation, and Development (NYHPD) issued a request for proposals for low-rise, two-family, market-rate housing for the Arverne Urban Renewal Area on the Rockaway Peninsula in Queens, a 308-acre site that is the largest developable tract of land in New York's five boroughs. The area is already home to more than 13,500 families in publicly funded buildings constructed between 1951 and 1974, during three different eras of public housing, but otherwise has remained undeveloped since it was cleared in the late 1960s. Earlier proposals ranged from plans to build as many as ten thousand units of low-income housing on the site, to a multimedia gaming park and hotel complex, but the current RFP calls for just twelve hundred units of housing on a hundred acres—a reduced density of eight to twelve units per acre—to be developed as market-rate rather than low-income housing. The NYHPD's goal is to distribute land held since the 1970s to public-private partnerships in a way that ultimately eliminates its own development role, and to reduce the concentration of low-income tenants created by earlier federal, state, and local initiatives.

What makes this new development significant is that it represents not only the intersection of the old and the new in federal housing but also a direct outgrowth of the *16 Houses* model of collaboration. The NYHPD and the Architectural League of New York produced a set of proposals for the site (in addition to the official proposals) that tested the potential of what was achieved in Houston. Four architectural teams offered ideas: CASE (Reninier de Graaf, Bruce Fisher, Beth Margulis, and John Bosch); Michael Sorkin Studio with Shop and SystemArchitects; Diana Balmori, Deborah Berke, Peggy Deamer, Keller Easterling; and my own firm, Michael Bell Architecture, directing the research and planning, and working with Marble Fairbanks Architects and Mark Rakatansky Studio on new housing prototypes.

One promising outcome is that the NYHPD is now considering hiring architects and planners *before* developers. By bringing architects into the process earlier, the agency could create a more level playing field where design would be better equipped to compete with finance—and the end result might be more options for the people who will actually use the new housing.

Notes

1. *Quality Housing and Work Responsibility Act of 1998,* 105th Cong., 2nd sess., H.R. 4194: The QHWRA amends the United States Housing Act of 1937 and attempts to help "eligible families make the transition from welfare to work." It allocated $283 million to public housing agencies for tenant-based assistance. Under Section 513 of the Act, "Income Targeting," the United States Housing Act of 1937 is amended to allow public housing agencies to "establish and utilize income-mix criteria for the selection of residents for dwelling units." A public housing agency cannot "concentrate very low-income families in public housing dwelling units in certain public housing projects or certain buildings within projects." The Act requires the creation of admissions policies "designed to provide for deconcentration of poverty and income-mixing bringing higher income tenants into lower income projects and lower income tenants into higher income projects." Incentives may be offered to tenants to move. The Act also requires that adult tenants contribute time to community service, and participate in economic self-sufficiency programs.

2. The National Alliance of HUD Tenants and ENPHRONT (National Public Housing Tenants Organization), "Report on the Loss of Subsidized Housing in the U.S." (October 4, 2002, <http://saveourhomes.org/Senate_Report.htm>).

3. The Fifth Ward lies to the northeast of downtown Houston. It is bordered by Buffalo Bayou and I-10 on the south. Settled after the Civil War by former slaves, it was once an official voting district. Today it is predominantly African American, but in 1866, the population was half white and half African American, and two segregated schools served the neighborhood. Churches have played an important role in the Fifth Ward's social and political life since its founding. Mount Vernon United Methodist Church, established in 1865 by former slave Toby Gregg, is the oldest church in the area, but Pleasant Grove Baptist, Mount Pleasant Baptist, Sloan Memorial United Methodist, Payne Chapel Methodist, and First Shiloh Baptist are all also over a hundred years old. The Fifth Ward flourished at the end of the nineteenth century as the Southern Pacific Railroad became a source of income and jobs, and African American–owned businesses began to prosper early in the twentieth century. Lyons Avenue, the main street, was once known as the Harlem of the South, and remains the center of business and social life in the neighborhood.
   Despite revitalization efforts, the Fifth Ward, which has a population of approximately eighteen thousand, still faces serious challenges: The number of residents over the age of sixty-five is more than twice the city average, and the working-age population faces high unemployment rates. The current revitalization is in part based in the area's rich history. Former residents include Barbara Jordan, the first black congresswoman from the South, and Ruth Simmons, former president of Smith College. The Fifth Ward is also home to civil rights pioneer Lonnie Smith, whose 1944 Supreme Court case opened Southern primaries to African Americans. Diana J. Kleiner, "Fifth Ward, Houston," *Handbook of Texas Online,* <www.tsha.utexas.edu/handbook/online/articles/view/F F/hpfhk.html>, and Fifth Ward Community Redevelopment Corporation, "Mission Statement" (Fifth Ward Community Redevelopment Corporation, Houston, Texas, n.d.).

4. According to Lawrence Anderson, William W. Wurster's directives while dean of the MIT School of Architecture and Planning separated the concerns of planning and architecture. Planning faculty were not trained in design but in economics and public policy; the planning department produced analysts, public-policy makers, and activists, and the architecture department focused on training designers. See Anderson, *Inside the Large Small House: The Residential Design Legacy of William W. Wurster,* ed. R. Thomas Hille (New York: Princeton Architectural Press, 1994), 10.

5. Michael Bell, "Having Heard Mathematics: The Topologies of Boxing," and Michael Bell and Sze Tsung Leong, "347 Years: Slow Space," in *Slow Space,* ed. Michael Bell and Sze Tsung Leong (New York: The Monacelli Press, 1998), 22, 107. Peter Eisenman's analysis of Giuseppe Terragni's Casa Giuliani-Frigerio includes a description of the spatial ambiguity developed from two opposing concepts of space in Terragni's work. Terragni's architecture was ultimately understood to encapsulate an expansion and contraction of two types of space or the simultaneity of centrifugal and centripetal space. *16 Houses* applies this work to the analysis of federal housing policy and recent goals of decentralization.

6. Sanford Kwinter, "Playboys of the Western World," *ANY*, 13 (1996): 62.

7. K. Michael Hays, "Introduction," *Architecture Theory Since 1968*, ed. K. Michael Hays (Cambridge, Mass.: MIT Press, 1998), xiv.

8. Curtis Lang, "A Depleted Legacy, Public Housing in Houston," *Cite* 33 (fall 1995–winter 1996): 10.

9. These projects reflect a general strain of urban work that does not easily resolve or give closure to urban crisis. I refer to the Internationale Bauausstellung Berlin. Peter Eisenman confronted the I.B.A. prerogatives by refusing to provide the perimeter block housing that was the norm in most I.B.A. projects: "The organizers of the I.B.A. wanted us to close the corner and make a contextual building. The question is, what is a contextual building here—what does closing a corner mean? First, it means covering up walls that have the scars of Berlin's history, of the bombings of World War II." Alan Balfour, *Berlin: The Politics of Order* (New York: Rizzoli, 1990), 235.

10. Kenneth Frampton, "The New Objectivity: Germany, Holland, and Switzerland, 1923–33," *Modern Architecture: A Critical History* (London: Thames and Hudson, 1985), 140. Walter Gropius wrote in *The Sociological Basis of Minimum Housing* (1929), "Since Technology operates within the framework of industry and finance and since any cost reduction achieved must first of all be exploited for the benefit of private industry, it will only be able to provide cheaper and more varied dwelling if the government increases private industry's interest in dwelling construction by increased welfare measures. If the minimum dwelling is to be realized at rent levels which the population can afford, the government must be requested to: (1) prevent waste of public funds for apartments of excessive size . . . for which an upper limit of apartment size must be established; (2) reduce the initial costs of roads and utilities; (3) provide the building sites and remove them from the hands of speculators; (4) liberalize as far as possible the zoning regulations and building codes."

11. Marc F. Plattner, "Democracy and the Acquisitive Spirit," in *South Africa's Crisis of Constitutional Democracy: Can the U.S. Constitution Help?,* ed. Robert A. Licht and Bertus de Villiers (Washington, D.C.: American Enterprise Institute Press), 114. See also Thomas Jefferson quoted in Plattner, 114: "The first principle of association guarantees the 'free exercise of [one's] industry and the fruits acquired by it.'"

12. Plattner, "Democracy and the Acquisitive Spirit," 121.

13. Félix Guattari, "Regimes, Pathways, Subjects," in *Incorporations,* ed. Jonathan Crary and Sanford Kwinter (New York: Zone Books, 1992), 21: "The new capitalist passion would sweep up everything in its path . . . The spirit of enlightenment, which marked the advent of this second figure of capitalist subjectivity, is necessarily accompanied by an utterly hopeless fetishization of profit."

14. Plattner, "Democracy and the Acquisitive Spirit," 119: "By making the political process rather than the 'honest industry' of private individuals the arbiter of each person's income, redistribution undermines the notion of genuinely private property. For the implicit assumption of such a policy is that a society's wealth is the sum of the wealth of its individual citizens, but that each individual's wealth is merely the share of the society's wealth that government decides to allot them. By making everyone's income directly dependent on governmental largesse, a policy of explicit redistribution must necessarily politicize society. In effect, each citizen would become the equivalent of a government grantee or a welfare recipient, and it is hard to see how anyone could hope to avoid the government's solicitude about how he or she was spending the public's money . . . It seems unlikely, therefore, that a redistributionist society could maintain the protection of the private sphere necessary for personal liberty to flourish."

15. Henri Bergson, *Matter and Memory* (New York: Zone Books, 1988), 23. Bergson uses the word "intuition" to refer to that which transcends the relativity of knowing something by translation or representation. Movement outside of and around the object—in this case, the city—is composed of simultaneous and multiple reconstructions of the object from an infinite number of vantage points: "By intuition is meant the kind of intellectual sympathy by which one places oneself within an object in order to coincide with what is unique to it."

16. Bergson, *Matter and Memory,* 9.

17. Bergson, *Matter and Memory,* 9.

18. Henri Bergson, *An Introduction to Metaphysics* (New York: Knickerbocker Press, 1912), 23.

19. Robert A. Caro, *The Power Broker* (New York: Vintage Books, 1975), 611.

20. Caro, *Power Broker*, 611.

21. Caro, *Power Broker,* 611. In invitational materials given to the architects of *16 Houses* at the outset of the design process, Butler's words served as a precursor to comments by Michel Foucault: "If one were to find a place, and perhaps there is someplace, where liberty is effectively exercised, one would find that this is not owing to the order of the objects, but, once again, owing to the practice of liberty. Which is not to say that, after all, one may as well leave people in slums, thinking that they can simply exercise their rights to freedom." *The Foucault Reader,* ed. Paul Rabinow (New York: Pantheon Books, 1984), 199.

22. Caro, *Power Broker,* 611.

23. Vanessa Gallman, "Government Will Raze 70,000 more HUD Units," *Houston Chronicle*, May 31, 1996, 6A.

24. *Foucault Reader,* Rabinow, 199.

25. See New York City Housing Authority, "Fact Sheet" (New York City Housing Authority, November 25, 2002, <http://www.nyc.gov/html/nycha/pdf/factsheet.pdf>): The New York City Housing Authority (NYCHA) provides affordable housing for low-income city residents. The Authority currently manages and maintains 345 public housing developments, with 2,702 residential buildings that have 181,000 units housing nearly 535,000 residents, including an estimated 105,000 persons living doubled up. In addition, through the federally funded Section 8 Existing Housing Program, NYCHA uses certificates and vouchers to assist an additional 77,000 families in private apartments. The Authority manages new construction and rehabilitation of public housing buildings and units. While continuing to maintain a safe and secure living environment in its public housing developments, the Authority also focuses on providing social services for the needs of its residents.

26. Neal MacFarquhar, "U.S. Getting Public Housing Closer to the Ground," *New York Times*, June 2, 1996, 1A.

27. This estimate is based only on the value of the vouchers and does not include administrative costs.

28. Texas Department of Transportation information gathered from T.D.O.T. web site.

29. The freeway cost estimate is for an eight- to ten-lane portion of Texas I-8. The estimate is based on a 7.97-mile stretch of mostly concrete pavement. The construction contract was for a period of approximately one year, from March 1993 to October 1994. The final cost is estimated at $182,824,356. Another segment of freeway built the same year, State Highway 99, was estimated at $3,850,000 per mile, or a total cost of $63,220,000 for a 16.42-mile segment of four to six lanes. The total personal income for Harris County in 1995 was $77,774,000,000.

30. Equity and mortgage payments based on a $50,000 loan at 7.9 percent for thirty years.

31. Equity and payment based on a $25,000 loan at 7.9 percent for five years.

32. The average weekly wage in Harris County in 1992 was $554.03; advertised mortgages on Sable Ridge homes were approximately $550 per month.

33. This estimate assumes that a downtown building could be built for the same cost as the subdivision.

34. Adam Smith, *An Inquiry into the Nature and Causes of the Wealth of Nations* (1789), ed. Edwin Cannan (New York: Random House, 1937), 5: In 1776, Adam Smith in the *Wealth of Nations* defined the way the division of labor produced surplus. The theory is simple in concept, but its implications are dramatic, especially when they bear on the market production of individual houses, as they do in the United States. Smith used an example to describe the surplus value added by divided labor processes: ten men or women working in unison in a manner that divided the fabrication into discrete segments could produce an exponential multiple of what could be produced by a single person working alone. The division of labor gives each worker a "peculiar" task, as Smith says, that is odd in its separation from the whole—when his or her labor is combined with the labor of other workers, it ideally produces a unified project. Smith's example is that of pin-making in 1776. He shows how ten workers together can assemble forty-eight thousand pins in one day, while a lone worker could "scarcely produce 20 pins." Two issues surface in Smith's explanation. First, if ten workers can produce forty-eight thousand pins in a day, can one man or woman say he or she has to his or her credit forty-eight hundred

pins or one-tenth of the total? Can a single worker claim his proportional share of the total even if his work has been exponentially compounded by the division of labor? Second, in Smith's use of the word "peculiar," he refers to work that is taken out of a complete and grounding context. For example, a worker may have no other task than to sharpen the end of the wire used in pin-making, and this task may be completed in isolation of the entire project. The word peculiar evolves into the more resonant and complex term "alienation" in later examinations of labor by Karl Marx and Guy Debord.

35. See Moishe Postone, *Time, Labor, and Social Domination* (Cambridge: Cambridge University Press, 1993), 294: The division of labor and its territorial relation to production is enunciated in a renewed form. The city as a site of labor is understood to have become a territorial entity capable of sustaining the advantages of divided labor and the familial territory of preindustrial labor: "The city economy was in the lucky situation of being able to enjoy the advantages of the division of labor without losing the feeling . . . of familial origins. One worked in the city and for the city; life moved in a circle . . . that made the city a center of interests that could be clearly surveyed. Everyone could perceive the totality, and therefore everyone took part in the prosperity of the whole . . . In the city economy, production and trade dealt with objects that functioned as carriers of common spirit, and that spirit too constituted prosperity. In the capitalist world economy, however, the sense of economic connection . . . has been lost: The industrial workers who fill the new quarters (of the city) work to satisfy needs that arise somewhere far distant in the country of even beyond borders: they work essentially for distant markets, for unknown customers, and not as a city dweller for a city dweller . . . They cannot perceive the effects of their activity within the city economy."

36. See Thomas Jefferson quoted in Plattner, "Democracy and the Acquisitive Spirit," 114: "To take from one, because it is thought his own industry and that of his fathers, has acquired too much, in order to spare others, who, or whose fathers have not exercised equal industry or skill, is to violate arbitrarily the first principle of association."

37. Postone, *Time, Labor, and Social Domination*, 181.
38. Postone, *Time, Labor, and Social Domination*, 181.
39. Massimo Cacciari, *Architecture and Nihilism: On the Philosophy of Modern Architecture* (New Haven: Yale University Press, 1993), 187.
40. Cacciari, *Architecture and Nihilism*, 187.
41. *Foucault Reader,* Rabinow, 199: "Disciplinary power on the other hand is exercised through invisibility; at the same time it imposes on those whom it subjects a principle of compulsory visibility. In discipline, it is the subjects who have to be seen. Their visibility assures the hold of the power that is exercised over them. It is the fact of being constantly seen, of being able always to be seen, that maintains the disciplined individual in his subjection. And the examination is the technique by which power, instead of emitting the signs of its potency, instead of imposing its mark on its subjects, holds them in a mechanism of objectification. In this space of domination, disciplinary power manifests its potency, essentially by arranging objects. The examination is, as it were, the ceremony of this objectification."
42. David B. Brownlee and David G. DeLong, "Adventures of Unexplored Places: Defining a Philosophy, 1901–51," in *Louis Kahn, In the Realm of Architecture* (New York: Rizzoli, 1991), 42.
43. Theodor W. Adorno, *Negative Dialectics* (New York: Continuum, 1995), 231.
44. *Foucault Reader,* Rabinow, 247.
45. *Foucault Reader,* Rabinow, 245–47.

Entry vestibule, *16 Houses: Owning a House in the City*

16 Houses Exhibition Projects

The following projects are accompanied by statements written by the architects and/or collaborating artists.

Appel   Interloop   StudioWorks   Bell   Standard   Brown   Jiménez

Lerup, Hood & Thumb

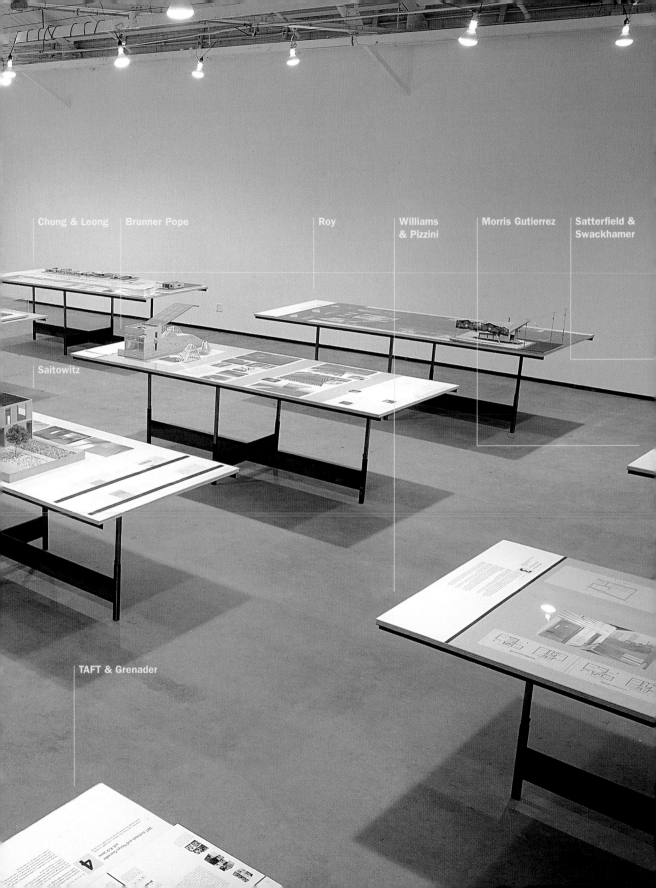

Chung & Leong | Brunner Pope

Roy

Williams & Pizzini

Morris Gutierrez

Satterfield & Swackhamer

Saitowitz

TAFT & Grenader

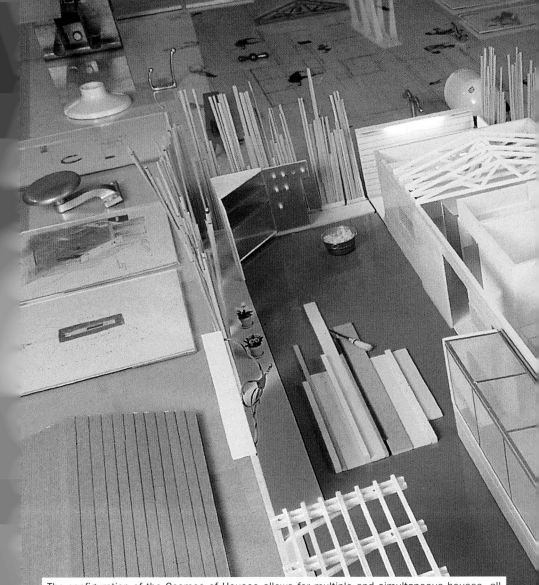

The configuration of the Cosmos of Houses allows for multiple and simultaneous houses, all for the same family, all on the same lot. This spatial maneuver provides more space on the same piece of land. The major components of the Cosmos of Houses are the Inside House inside the Outside House inside the Inside-Outside House. Finer layers of the multiple and simultaneous houses include the Bow-Wow House inside the Outside House, the Green Side Line House inside the Inside-Outside House and beside the Outside House, and the Miniature Scale Model House, which finds its home inside the home itself.

The Inside-Outside House occupies the entire lot. "Within" this Inside-Outside House, the outside land, or yard, becomes a new inside. It is populated with helpful apparatuses and furniture—an oversized table that creates shade, a corner cupboard, several sinks, perimeter lighting, chairs on feet that do not sink into the mud, but encourage occupation and facilitate the transformation from outside to inside.

The Outside House is a reinterpretation of the single-family American object house. It has a front porch; its walls divide (with slippages) the inside from the outside and determine what are seen as the side, front, and backyards.

The Inside House is nestled, or nested, into the wrappers of the Inside-Outside House and the Outside House. It is another interpretation of the standard American house, turned 180 degrees so that a second "front" yard is superimposed upon the backyard of the Outside House.

double barrel

The simultaneity of these houses creates expanded spatial opportunities. The master bedroom, for example, occupies a number of spaces simultaneously. In the world of the Inside House, the master bedroom is the front porch, and the bed sits under the porch canopy contained within the perimeter of the Outside House. It faces onto the front yard of the Inside House, which sits within and over the backyard of the Outside House. In the Inside-Outside House, the master bedroom begins at the wall of the Inside House, extends through the space of the Outside House, and terminates at the back property line, where a grooming sink is built into the self-growing cabinetry of the hedgerow. A pivot door, which is a piece of the Outside House wall, opens ninety degrees, taking with it a shelf and seat; in this position, it becomes the wall of the iteration of the master bedroom that occupies the footprint of the Inside-Outside House as it extends to the property line. Finally, in its most normative, comfortable position, the master bedroom is simply the rearmost space in the Outside House, fronting on the backyard.

Materials and methods include the most standard and economical existing or found raw bulk materials, such as Hardiplank and Hardipanel fiber-cement siding, multiple-density fiberboard, concrete slab on grade, concrete block, Thermoclear double-wall structural plastic, wood trusses, windowpane glass, drywall, and United Greenhouse Systems standard parts. Carefully chosen accouterments and additives accessorize the standard materials: a 96¢ cast-plastic lamp base, a 75¢ cast-aluminum door handle, paint, and concrete stain.

Some Directives for Moving into (This) Next Century, or You Can't Go Wrong (But It's Hard to Go Right)

The city as a physical artifact dominates our perception. It is characterized by the expression of dominant forces and by the suppression of other stealthier, subtler forces. Building the city starts with enthusiasm, develops through complex forces, then comes to a stop. It reaches a position of completion and is hard to change.

The large-scale projects—often utopian in spirit—have failed. The last freeway in a city has been constructed. The land has been used up. The city has spread past its useful limits. Visionary proposals have ground to a halt.

Perhaps the city is not a single entity. Perhaps we need more names for cities so that their differences can emerge. Perhaps the city is really fifty-five cities, or fifty-five versions of fifty-five cities. Perhaps the city is really many cities layered, formed, and reformed through everyday use.

Everyone has a role in making and remaking the future city. Designers need to strip away the layers of preconception and enjoy the messy foray into the future. They can no longer work on the whole.

The whole does not exist. Participant-defined wholes or cities within the non-city are perhaps where the action is.

And you can't go wrong (but it's hard to go right).

PROJECT TEAM: SUNG CHO, FEDERICO DEVERA, JASON ETHERIDGE, EDWARD KIM

No need to knock.

The house
in both
plan and section
weaves and folds
inside and out
over and under
in front and behind.

This double terrain,
a tube unwinding on itself,
shades and views
landscape and skyscape.
Looking at itself
through itself
from itself,
making places to hide
and peep.

This double terrain,
the house raised
above the ground,
doubles the space
for dwelling,
inside causing out.

A path from front to rear
measures the site and
becomes the porch,
turned to the street,
organizing the rooms
and courts
into the street,
organizing the rooms
and courts
into the site,
making a frame that
views back to the front.

The material
of the traditional roof
is used to construct
volume,
providing space without square feet.
Volume,
and the porch,
and the fans,
allow natural cooling.

The bathroom
is family style.
Park below,
BBQ next to,
live in front,
cook behind,
eat alongside,
sleep above,
garden around.
Sit under a bedroom
or tree.

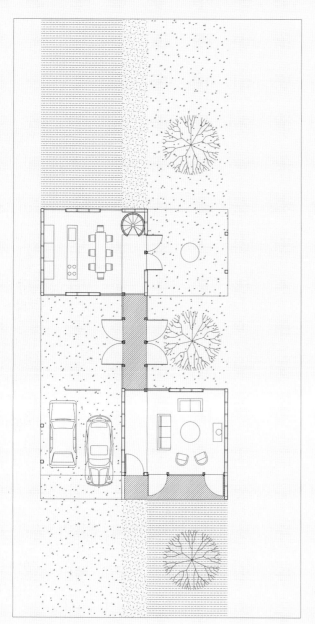

First-floor plan

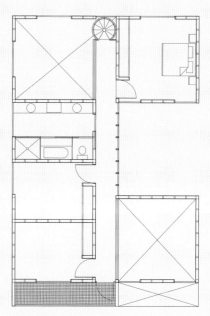

Second-floor plan

DOMESTIC TOPOGRAPHIC PACKAGE KEITH KRUMWIEDE (STANDARD)

WITH CAROL TREADWELL

PROJECT TEAM: ANDREW ALBERS, WILLIAM HALL, BRIAN HEISS, MATTHEW SELTZER, MARY SPRINGER, WITH LYNN FISHER, MICHAEL SWEEBE

This project questions the acceptance of the typical single-family house as a one-size-fits-all solution to the problem of housing, offering an organizational system that facilitates choice and change while providing the necessary support for living and the surfaces it requires. The architects take up the challenge of constructing the house as a unit of mass production (which is made affordable through economies of scale using short-run prefabricated building methods) to generate a flexible domestic environment that transcends the systemization of its construction. The house is responsive to both the ever-changing demands of family life and the unique climatic conditions of Houston.

Liz woul[...]
rig up c[...]
th[...]

The design breaks the conventional single-family house open and pulls it up and across three levels to construct a fluid domestic topography at the scale of the site. Each level of the house is linked to the others through various openings and material continuities (or slipped surfaces) that integrate the house across the section, generating a variably dense and expansive interior that capitalizes on the interconnectedness of different areas of family life. The ground level consists of a series of overlapping outdoor rooms, porches, and gardens around a central indoor-outdoor room. The upper levels of the house narrow to twelve feet wide and float above the ground, taking advantage of the natural cooling potential of the winds and engaging the tree canopy as an extension of the interior. The traditional rooms are arranged to provide for varying degrees of privacy and openness. The planning and sectional organization of the house—combined with strategically choreographed views and adjacencies, material shifts, cabinet inserts, and moving panels (doors that operate at the scale of a wall)—allow its spaces to be discrete yet adaptable.

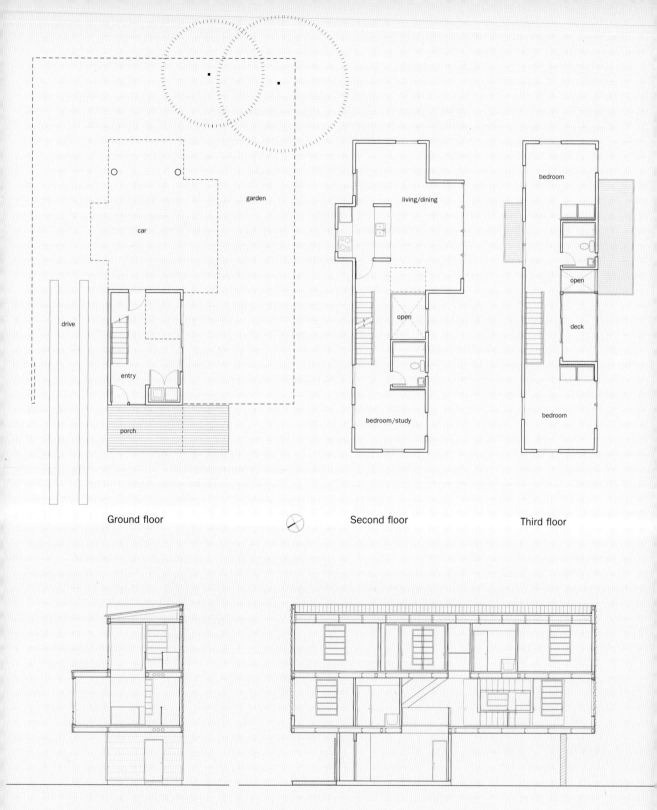

garden

car

drive

entry

porch

living/dining

open

bedroom/study

bedroom

open

deck

bedroom

Ground floor

Second floor

Third floor

Plug-in scenarios

Plan variants

On Sundays during football season, Dad would drag the TV out onto the deck. Mom would say, "That thing'll kill the plants!" But secretly she was fine with Dad getting a little fresh air. I worried that the neighbors would complain—when the Saints scored (or got scored on!) his voice could really sail—but Liz just shrugged. She was surprisingly accommodating, really, if Dad wanted to make a scene one day a week, though the deck tended to be her domain. She was happy to take refuge under a tree with a chair and her book (as long as she could find some bug repellent). "Quietude the old-fashioned way" was what she called it.

Sometimes in the afternoon, Mom would say, "I think I'll go relax in my ultra-private, ultra-luxurious, utterly faraway, top-secret-location, no-room-number-to-give-it-away hotel room." And then she'd disappear up the stairs and behind her door, leaving Liz and me staring after her and then at each other. Sometimes I'd make the universal sign for crazy, circling my finger beside my ear. But we knew there was no point in knocking on her door, even if we wanted to tease her, because she believed what she said. She wouldn't have heard us if we'd banged as hard as we could.

Liz would sometimes get obsessed with crossword puzzles, and she'd station herself on the floor in the center of the house and yell through the holes, putting the whole house to work for her. "Four letters, second one's a *p*, the clue is 'loyal.' "

"All right," Dad would reply.

Mom would write it down and call reassuringly, "I'm thinking." And I, personally, would hear the voice of a strange and arbitrary god, sometimes coming down from above, sometimes—suspiciously—up from below. Mom almost always said it was okay if we used the holes to yell through—it all depended on her mood. We tried to convince her that it was all one big room, that a room could be vertical as easily as it could be horizontal, that we were just calling across the room, that we really weren't "yelling through the house," which is funny because that's exactly what we were doing.

Liz invented the game where we lay down in the yard, staring up at the house. It could only be played during the day, when the windows reflected the sun and the whole house shone like one big wall, and we could pretend that it was a futuristic skyscraper, a gargantuan. We imagined that we were miles away, and that below the building walked pedestrians no bigger than the tips of our fingers. We pretended that birds landing on the roof were airplanes and helicopters in disguise. And sometimes we pretended that we were a rival power, planning an assault on the seemingly invincible facade. We said we'd wait until nightfall, when the windows would reappear. Then we'd send in our reconnaissance team to scale the walls and get a good look at what, in that building, those mysterious people really had going on.

—**Carol Treadwell**

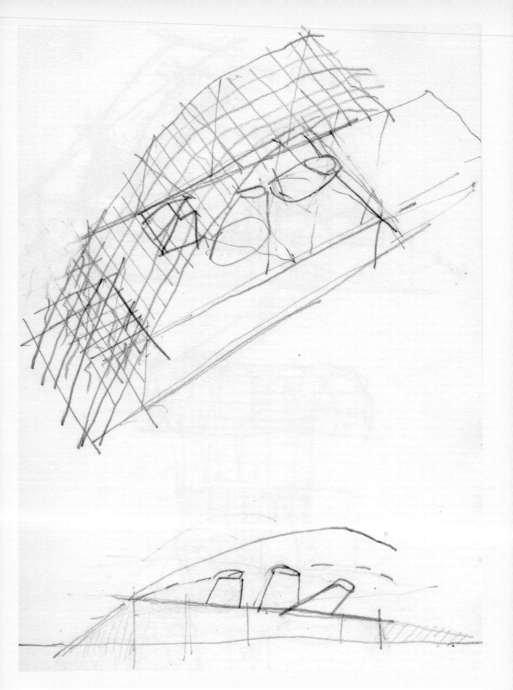

The fortress subdivision and house are characteristic of Houston. Manifestations of these barricaded domestic settings—closed gate, chain-link fence, armed guard, dead bolt, rottweiler, windowless walls, burglar bars, alarm systems, razor wire, club, family handgun—show only signs of increasing fortification to the point of virtual imprisonment.

The spontaneous street life of the Fifth Ward is an anomaly given the near complete privatization of the Houston street. This project attempts to learn from the Fifth Ward, demonstrating an alternative to the house as defensive fortification.

Here, public space is invaded by intimate space. A still-vibrant private world is enlisted in the relief of a hopelessly broken public world. In this regard, it is important to remember that the dead and hostile Houston street is not the cause of barricaded privacy—it is the effect of barricaded privacy.

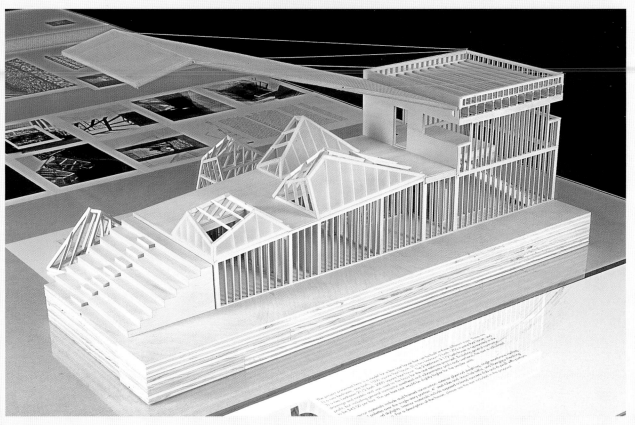

One significant feature of the house is a single-story portion of its roof given over to the street. Bermed steps starting at the front property line pull the street space a full seventy feet into the site, forming a crossover section where public roofscape and private, ground-floor living zones overlap, creating a site for interrelations. This site is animated by two architectural features. The first is a four-inch steel-tube canopy supporting a chain-link trellis that will be planted with vines. The second comprises three large wood-framed skylights sheathed in translucent fiberglass, which bring in light and extend the space of the bedroom and bathroom below, cautiously breaching the most intimate recesses of the house.

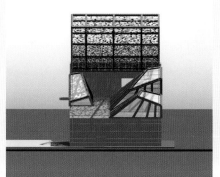 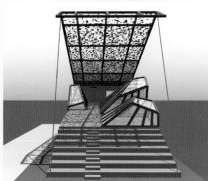 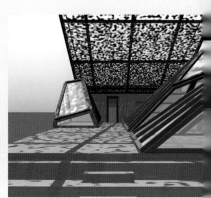

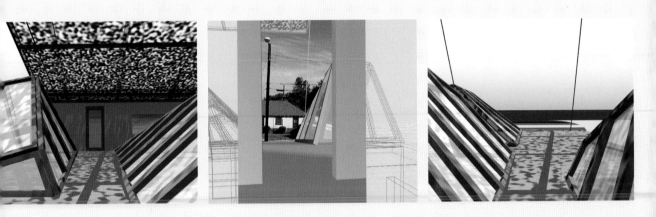

Two paths offer access to the house. The first leads up the bermed steps from the sidewalk, over the roof, and though the front door, which opens into a loft and the upper part of the living-dining space. Stairs immediately to the right descend to the public space of the house. A second and more direct means of entry goes from the driveway into a small vestibule that leads directly to the ground floor of the living-dining space. Adjacent to the living-dining room is an open kitchen with access to three private bedrooms and one and a half interconnected bathrooms.

Exterior materials include stud-framed construction, plywood sheathing, single-membrane roofing with wood palettes over the single-story portion, metal-tube and chain-link trellis, and fiberglass sheathing over skylights framed with four-by-fours. Among the interior materials are colored concrete slab and drywall with exposed framing.

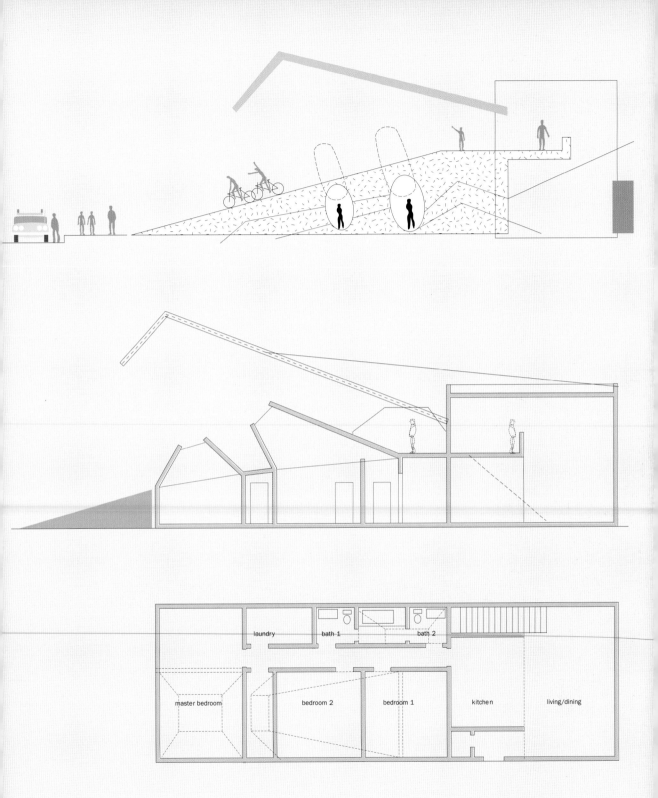

laundry · bath 1 · bath 2

master bedroom · bedroom 2 · bedroom 1 · kitchen · living/dining

Affordable housing should be understood as a commitment of time rather than simply an immediate solution to a pressing need. Eschewing the current fervor for disposability, and the swift and inevitable waste it entails, and departing from the low-cost model, the eleven-hundred-square-foot Peavy establishes a single-story model for expanding the life span, potential, and quality of the house beyond its economic limits.

Heritage Homes

THE PEAVY

3 Bedrooms
2 Baths
1,105 sq. ft.

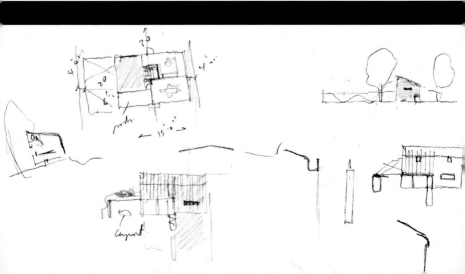

Rather than focusing solely on the pursuit of low-cost variables, the design attempts to develop an architecture that is compact and economical yet volumetrically expansive by deploying natural light—the richest and most optimistic of materials. It suggests that the typical oversized fifty-by-one-hundred-foot plot allotted to each house can be used as a field for cultivation of fruit or vegetables. The proposal promotes the idea of building with more durable and lasting materials (properly cured wood siding, concrete siding or block, stucco on lath, and metal) assembled with readily available technologies that result in a low-maintenance house that will last for decades. The final goal was to capitalize on the virtues of a palette of modest and simple elemental materials.

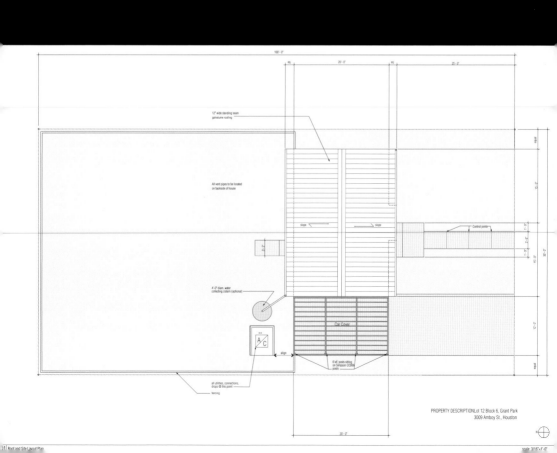

100'-0"

12" wide standing seam galvalume roofing

All vent pipes to be located on backside of house

slope   slope

Control joints

4'-0" diam. water collecting cistern (optional)

Car Cover

A/C

6"x6" posts sitting on Simpson CCB64 posts

all utilities, connections, drops @ this point

fencing

PROPERTY DESCRIPTION Lot 12 Block 6, Grant Park
3009 Amboy St., Houston

11 Roof and Site Layout Plan   scale 3/16"=1'-0"

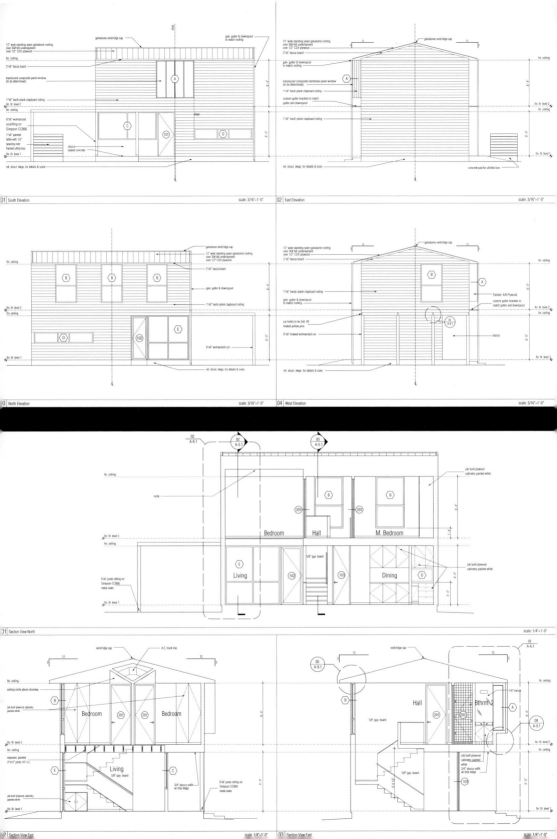

01 | South Elevation   scale: 3/16"=1'-0"

02 | East Elevation   scale: 3/16"=1'-0"

03 | North Elevation   scale: 3/16"=1'-0"

04 | West Elevation   scale: 3/16"=1'-0"

01 | Section View North   scale: 1/4"=1'-0"

02 | Section View East   scale: 1/4"=1'-0"

03 | Section View East   scale: 1/4"=1'-0"

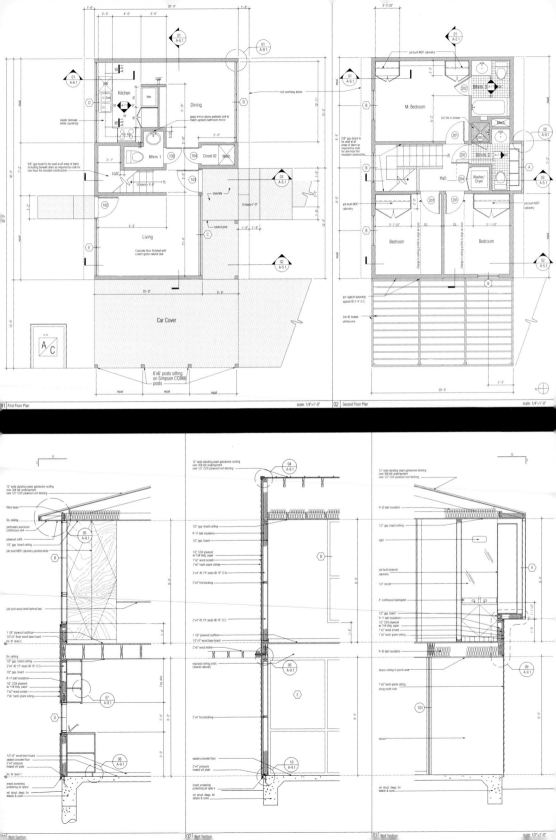

GAME HOUSE TAFT ARCHITECTS AND NONYA GRENADER WITH RICK LOWE

PROJECT TEAM: LENNY BREWER, JOHN CASBARIAN, CARLOS FIGHETTI, TIM GORDON, NONYA GRENADER, CHRIS KIMBALL, RICK LOWE, KIM NEUSCHELER, DANNY SAMUELS

Inspired by Charles and Ray Eames's Little Expandable House toy (1959), this project proposes a gaming strategy that uses a simple kit of parts to generate efficient, compact, low-cost house types with multiple options suited to individual needs and budgets. The basic enclosure is twenty by thirty-six feet (720 square feet). Twelve-foot walls create an attic that can be used for extra living and storage space (up to 432 additional square feet). Add-on parts include room additions, porches, carports or garages, stairs, and roof dormers. The compact size allows for more efficient land use, resulting in multiple units per lot.

The basic unit relies on a prefabricated kitchen-bathroom core that contains most of the complex and expensive components (mechanical, electrical, plumbing, cabinets, fixtures). The surrounding structure is built with appropriate on-site or prefabricated methods. Modular design options for floor, wall, and window panels offer choices of size, arrangement, orientation, view, and materials.

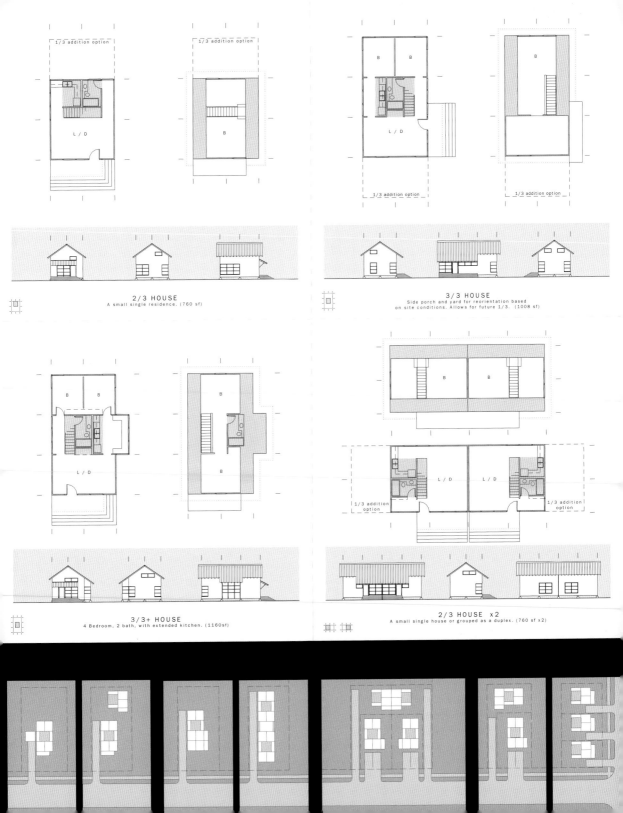

1/3 addition option   1/3 addition option

L / D

B

2/3 HOUSE
A small single residence. (760 sf)

B   B

B

L / D

1/3 addition option   1/3 addition option

3/3 HOUSE
Side porch and yard for reorientation based
on site conditions. Allows for future 1/3. (1008 sf)

B   B

B

L / D

B

3/3+ HOUSE
4 Bedroom, 2 bath, with extended kitchen. (1160sf)

B   B

L / D   L / D

1/3 addition
option

1/3 addition
option

2/3 HOUSE x2
A small single house or grouped as a duplex. (760 sf x2)

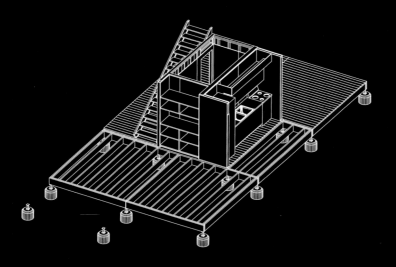

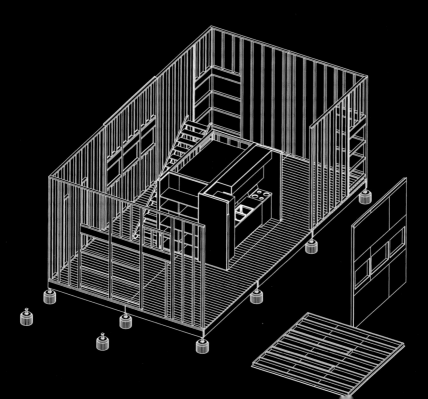

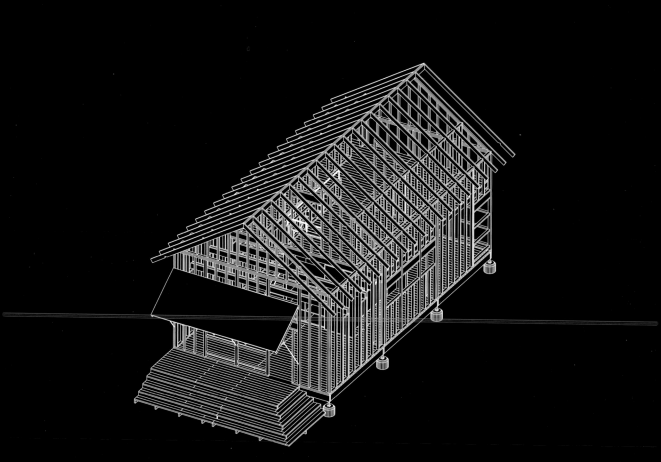

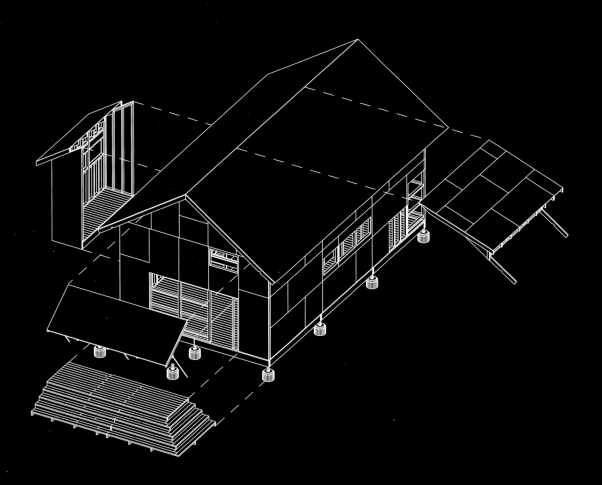

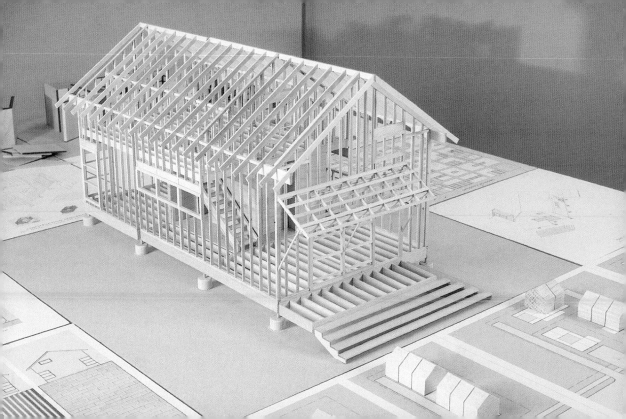

creates a crawl space that guarantees airflow under and between the exterior and interior skins of the house. A suspended scaffold allows ceiling fans to be hung at appropriate heights, augmenting cross-ventilation in the bedrooms. The scaffold extends to the street's edge, lighting the front porch, and out to a bug-zapper on the back porch. The sidewalk meets the recycling and garbage unit at the front wall of the kitchen. Adjacent houses share a common driveway.

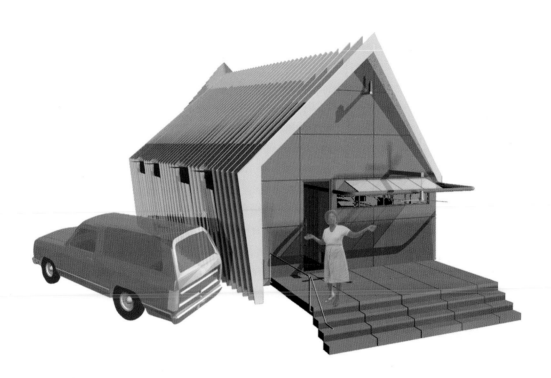

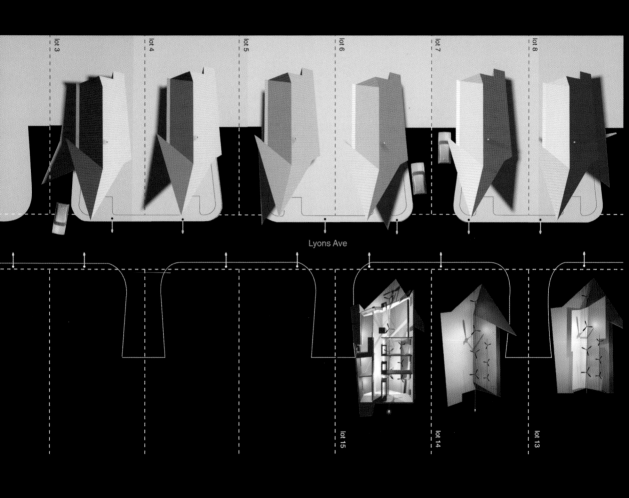

lot 3

lot 4

lot 5

lot 6

lot 7

lot 8

Lyons Ave

lot 15

lot 14

lot 13

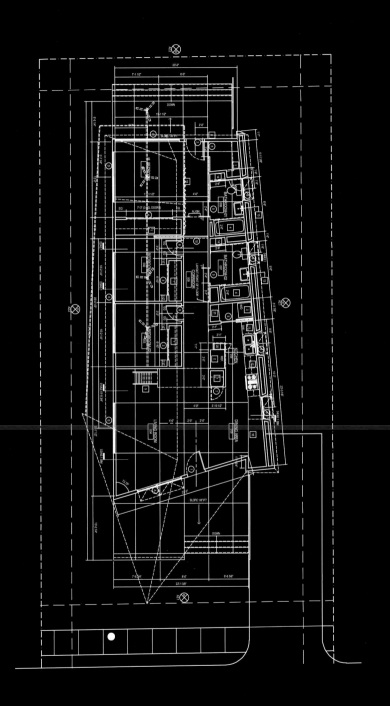

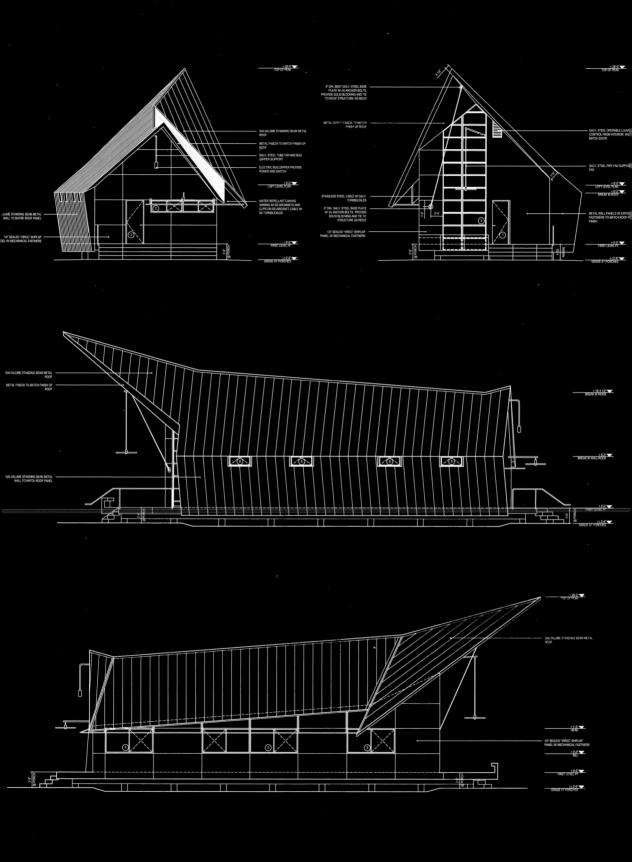

House lots in the Fifth Ward are large. Here, unlike many other communities in which affordable housing is a concern, land is not a major cost issue. This proposal takes advantage of the availability of outdoor space with a simple house and a spacious garden.

Gardens are not free, but with careful planning they can be started cheaply. They do not have to look complete on moving day. There is joy in marking tenure with a garden's progress.

Not every homeowner is a natural gardener, but this garden doesn't require a magic touch—the plants do not need a lot of watering, they stand up well to neglect, and they can survive Houston's extreme climate. Included in the proposal are alternatives for families with different skills and needs.

A garden is an investment in a community. This garden sits on the side of the house, facing the street. It is a very private garden with a very public face that occupants can adjust to the desired level of security and privacy.

The house employs some traditional Texan strategies for dealing with the climate—strategies that were more common before the invention of air-conditioning. The house has air-conditioning, but natural cooling will limit its use by a few weeks per year. The long, shaded, south-facing porch that links the garden to the main living spaces provides an enjoyable gathering space.

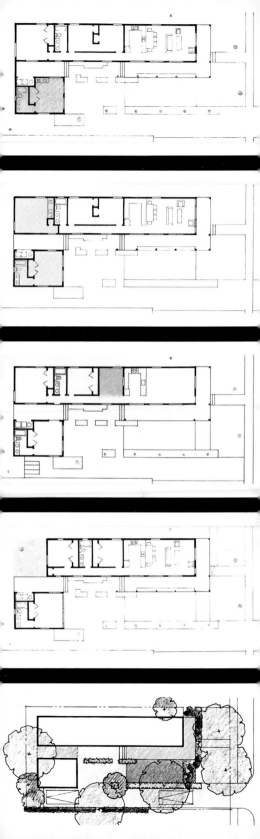

FIVE MODEL HOUSES NATALYE APPEL ARCHITECTS

WITH TRISH HERRERA AND RACHEL HECKER

PROJECT TEAM: LONNIE D. HOOGEBOOM, DONNA K. KACMAR, ROSANNE RAMOS, SHANNON B. SASSER, STUART SMITH

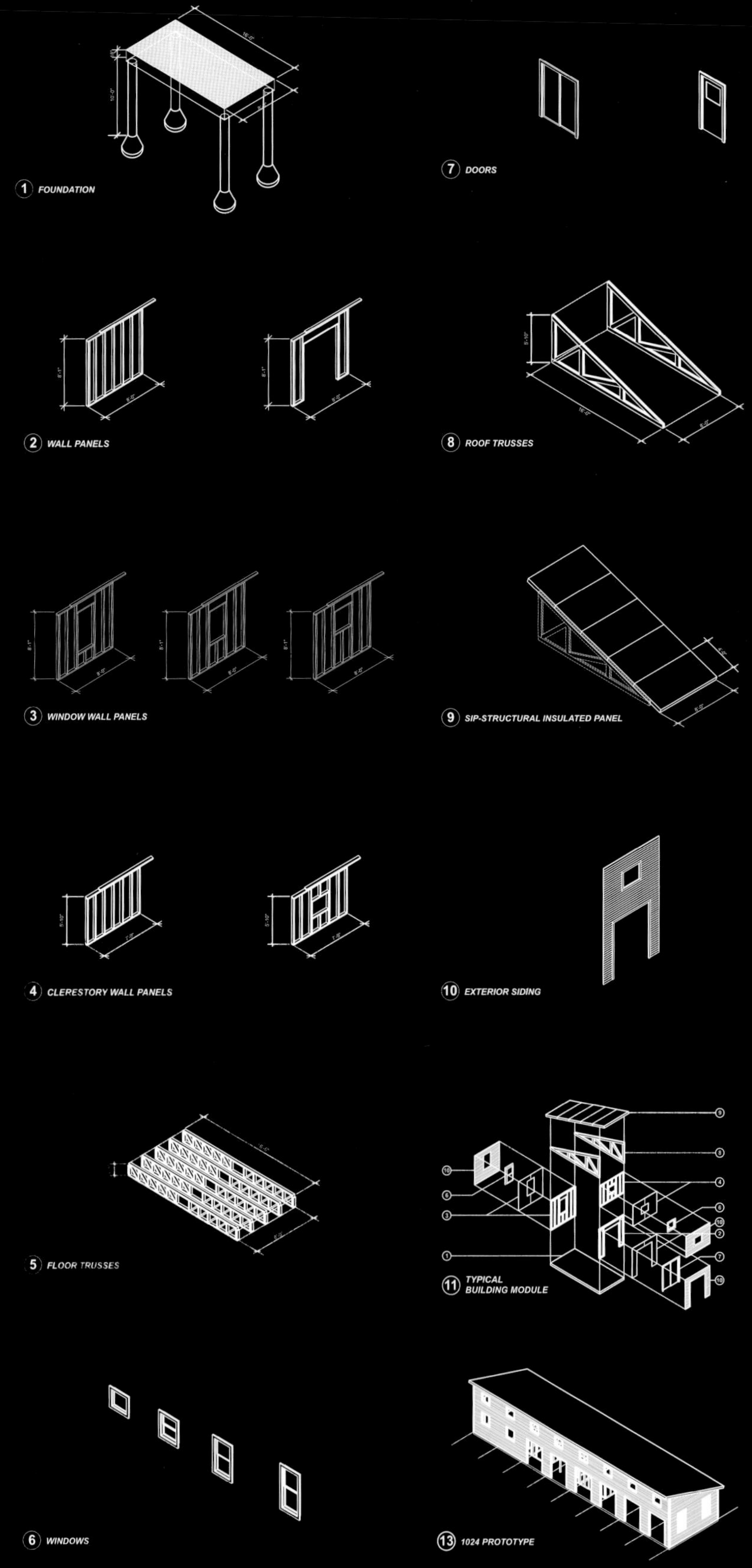

1 FOUNDATION

2 WALL PANELS

3 WINDOW WALL PANELS

4 CLERESTORY WALL PANELS

5 FLOOR TRUSSES

6 WINDOWS

7 DOORS

8 ROOF TRUSSES

9 SIP-STRUCTURAL INSULATED PANEL

10 EXTERIOR SIDING

11 TYPICAL BUILDING MODULE

13 1024 PROTOTYPE

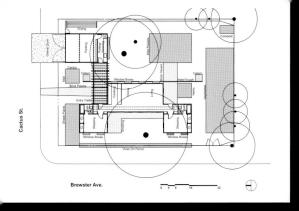

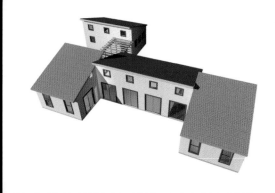

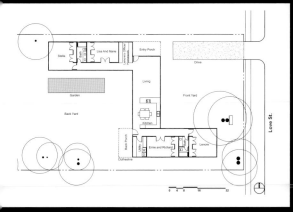

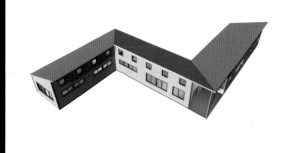

The projects are based on a system of prefabricated components with an eight-by-sixteen construction module. A typical bay is composed of two-by-four stud wall panels with sheathing, engineered floor joists, double roof trusses, and insulated structural roof panels. These components are erected on a concrete-slab foundation or raised concrete-block piers. Exterior finish materials are aluminum insulated windows, Hardiplank siding, and composition shingles. The modular components and conventional building materials offer an efficient and economical building system.

The design process began with the selection of potential sites in the Fifth Ward. The lots were identified by solar orientation, vegetation, and street relationships. The design of each of the five houses was inspired by a character from Trish Herrera's stories. The building system evolved to meet specific contextual and programmatic challenges. While the basic forms and materials of the five projects are similar, encouraging a sense of community and interconnectedness, each house reflects a high degree of individuality.

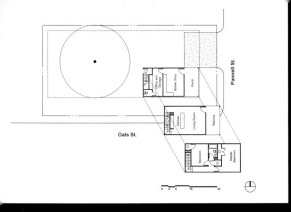

Sam's Barbershop was the oldest barbershop in the neighborhood. He started it in a little storefront on Lyons Avenue, but when he heard about the new houses being built he decided he wanted to have his own land. So he put his barbershop in part of his new house. Sam and his wife, Beatrice Jones, were delighted with their new home. Bea was a health-care worker who spent most of her days bathing and shopping for many of the elders in the neighborhood. Sam and Bea had been married thirty-five years and had never owned their own home until now. Somehow they never got around to having children, but they both felt like their children were the faces Sam had worked on for the last twenty-five years.

Sam spent long hours on his feet but never seemed tired. He loved a good game of poker. Sometimes he played with the new neighbor, James White, a Gulf War vet confined to a wheelchair and living on Social Security. The neighborhood poker games would start at three in the afternoon on Saturday and go until the next morning right before church.

"No gambling. Well, not much anyway," Sam confessed.

James had two sons—Steven, twelve, and Henry, fourteen. Steven had a paper route. He made good use of his bicycle, and he had some rollerblades too. In fact, Steven liked anything that rolled. Henry helped Sam clean up his barbershop after basketball practice. He yearned to make the varsity team in high school. He was a good player and had a shot at it.

"They're good boys," remarked Sam. "I know for a fact both of those boys give their dad some of their income to help pay for the new house."

Steven's paper route took him straight past Mrs. Guenther's house. Every morning when the sun was just rising, Mrs. Guenther was already awake feeding the stray cats in the neighborhood and watering her garden. Mrs. Guenther had moved into her new house a year and half ago, and already the vines she had planted were beginning to climb her roof. "Thank God for this rain," she said. As a girl, she grew up in the country and knew a lot about how to invite the earth to be part of her home, but after her husband died and her kids had grown up and moved away, she never dreamed she would be given another chance to have a garden.

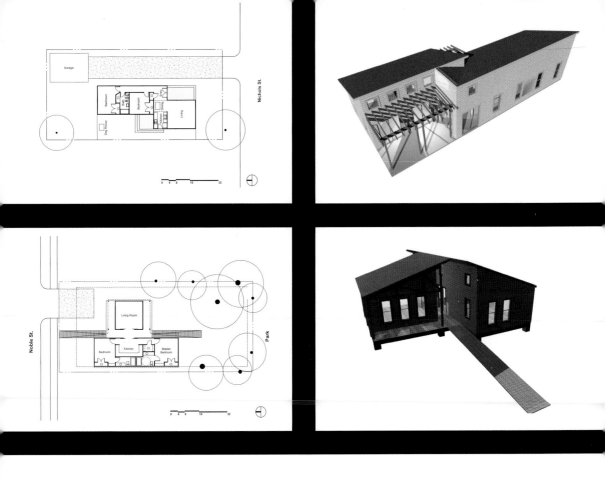

As Steven rolled by her house, Mrs. Guenther would wave him in for some cookies or rolls. She could dig in her garden, bake, and give advice all at the same time. "These cookies will give you the power to outlive even me," she'd say.

In the early 1900s, the Fifth Ward burned to the ground. At the time, Houston was segregated, and the Fifth Ward was home to African American people. Now people of every color adorn the neighborhood. It's a fast-growing area. The odd modern shapes of the new houses blend in with the older, colorful row houses, and with the new stadium coming up on the east side of downtown, there is promise of growth and activity and community that will last lifetimes.

—**Trish Herrera**

PROJECT TEAM: ALEX KNAPP (COMPUTER MODELING), BRETT BENSON AND JOSEPH GABRIEL (PH

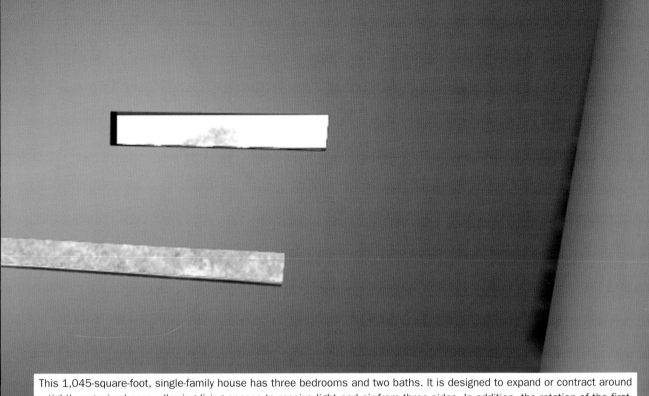

This 1,045-square-foot, single-family house has three bedrooms and two baths. It is designed to expand or contract around a tightly organized core, allowing living spaces to receive light and air from three sides. In addition, the rotation of the first- and second-floor plans around the core creates a generous porch on the front of the house and a carport in the back. On the second floor, the flipping produces a double-height space over the living room and a deck off the master bedroom.

Two types of economical windows built on site are important design features. The first is a long vertical window that fits conveniently between conventionally framed wood studs. The second is a horizontal fixed pane that sits between the framing and the partially removed siding.

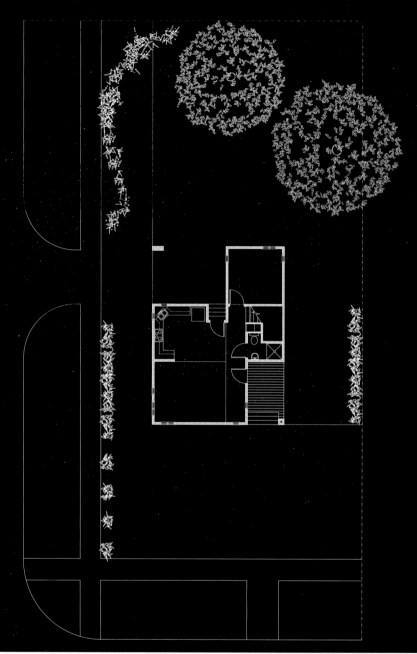

This design raises questions about approaches to affordable housing design. Attempts by architects to produce spatially flexible prefabricated houses typically benefit the fabricators more than the families for whom the houses are built. If the construction of affordable housing is considered an opportunity not only to produce buildings but to return capital to the community, then it becomes clear that the architect's role is to concentrate less on the structure as an assembly of components and more on the entire process, ensuring that manufacturing takes place locally so that the capital being spent does not leave the community.

Architects also often design spaces that dictate a lifestyle different from that of the residents, proposing houses that are unsuitable for the occupants' needs. While open plans are less expensive, for example, they may place a strain on a family with children of different ages. This house contains the traditional spaces necessary for a family. Economy is achieved through materials and design. Site-built construction—with wood-frame Hardiplank siding, asphalt shingle roofing, and tongue-in-groove pine decking flooring—is favored. The windows, in particular, are an attempt to free the project from the prefabrication process.

FIRST FLOOR

SECOND FLOOR

SECTION A - A1

SECTION B - B1

ELEVATION A

ELEVATION B

"Kneeling in the keeping room where she usually went to talk-think it was clear why Baby Suggs was so starved for color. There wasn't any except for two orange squares in a quilt that made the absence shout. The walls of the room were slate-colored, the floor earth-brown, the wooden dresser the color of itself, curtains white, and the dominating feature, the quilt over an iron cot, was made up of scraps of blue serge, black, brown and gray wool—the full range of the dark and the muted that thrift and modesty allowed. In that sober field, two patches of orange looked wild—like life in the raw."—Toni Morrison, *Beloved*

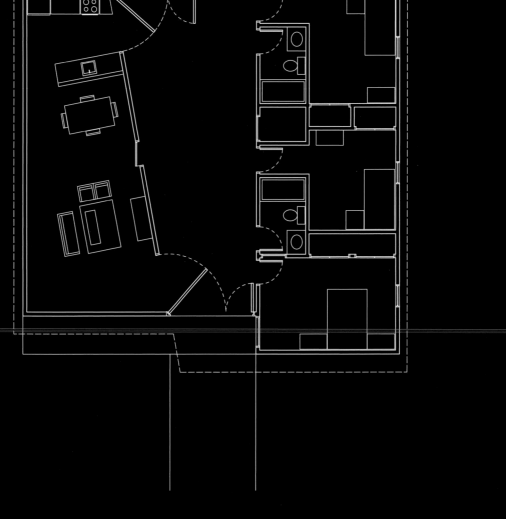

This project explores improvisation as a tactic for accepting limits and finding opportunities within them. A consideration of new materials that work with existing construction techniques and release the latent potential of wood-frame construction was essential to the design. Corrugated fiberglass siding combined with Plexiglas, colored acrylics, and sailcloth forms a low-cost cladding system with an inherent luminosity. Light may be admitted at any point between framing elements by cutting openings in the plywood and gypsum board and filling them with this cladding system.

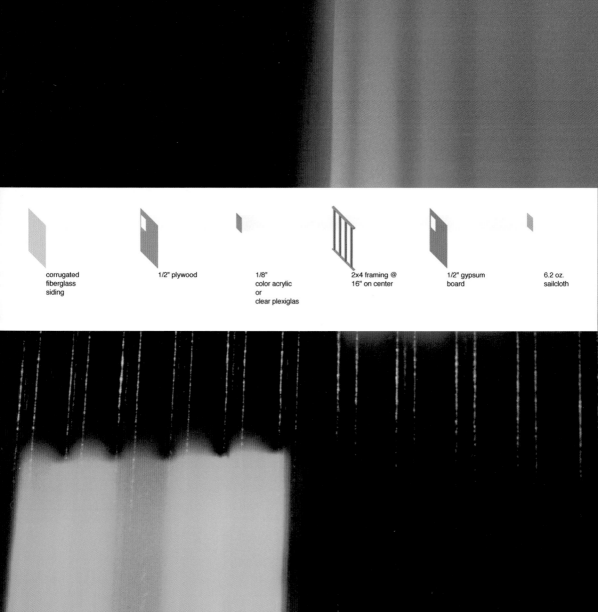

corrugated
fiberglass
siding

1/2" plywood

1/8"
color acrylic
or
clear plexiglas

2x4 framing @
16" on center

1/2" gypsum
board

6.2 oz.
sailcloth

In the film *Round Midnight*, Dexter Gordon's character, Dale Turner, discussing the music of Count Basie and Charlie Parker, offers, "I heard Lester Young and he sounded like he came out of the blue—because he was playing all the color tones, the sixths, the ninths, and major seventh, you know, like Debussy and Ravel." Such an interplay of sound and color informs the placement of the cladding panels. With a palette of color materials (two colors and clear) and frame sizes (eight-inch, sixteen-inch, and twenty-eight-by-sixteen-inch panels), the contractor acts as a composer and determines the phrasing of color in the spaces. The selection is comparable to the phrasing of chords in a musical composition.

This system allows the house to modulate the light of Houston's sky. A visual connection to its changing conditions is established with conventional north-facing windows in the open central space. When the doors are open, the space is comfortably ventilated and connects with the community of the Fifth Ward.

The idea of a low-cost house seems as though it should be anathema to a society that holds two-thirds of the world's wealth, particularly since the contradictions between the ideal and the real engender a certain skepticism about whether low-cost could ever be a rubric for a comfortable house. In a house for a client with limited means, design issues are complicated: One solution is to design a house that appeals to a wide range of individuals. It is a simple house, because living simply in an increasingly complex world has its virtues. The plan and organization do not rely on old stereotypes but suggest that private and public space are absolute needs. The private space is very private, while the public space is open to many uses: eating, entertaining, relaxing, snoozing, arguing, playing, dancing, laughing.

The first phase consists of a simple shed with bathroom and kitchen equipment. Gradually added to the shed are rooms that peek out from under the roof to join the canopy of trees typical of Houston's inner loop. The slight mimicry of the surrounding trees hints at the possibility of fusion between house and landscape.

The rooms added to the shed and the slogans on the wall are directed at imagined audiences: the metropolis, neighbors, and nature. Such writing on the wall has a long history in the American landscape, but it is usually associated with commercial establishments, from the corner store to roadside billboards. The idea of a speaking house is latent in the display of living rooms through plate-glass windows, the display of cars in large garages, and the display of planting on the front lawn. Here the step to direct communication is complete.

S-SPACE

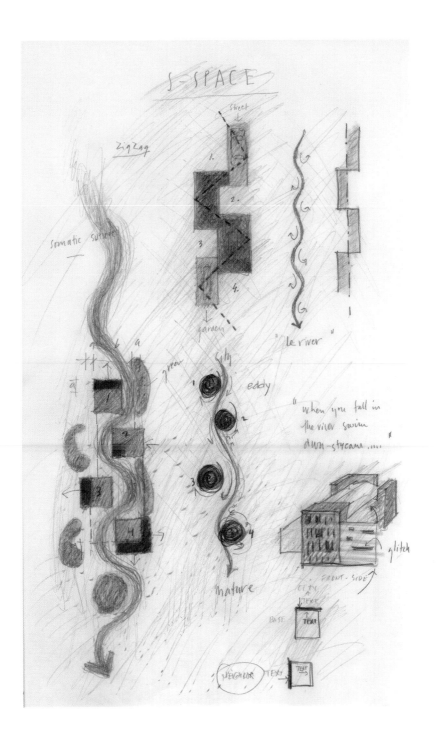

ZigZag

somatic suture

street ↓

1.

2.

3.

4.

garden ↓

green   silty

eddy

"le river"

"when you fall in
the river swim
down-stream ...."

mature

glitch

FRONT-SIDE →

CITY
↑ TEXT

BASE   TEXT

NEIGHBOR   TEXT

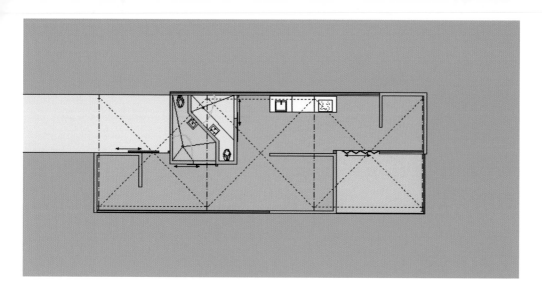

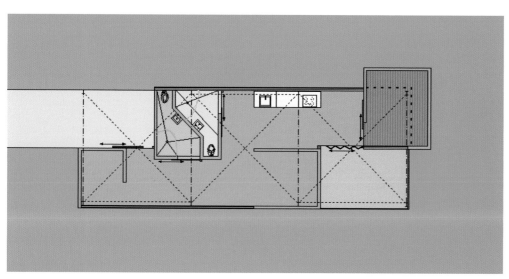

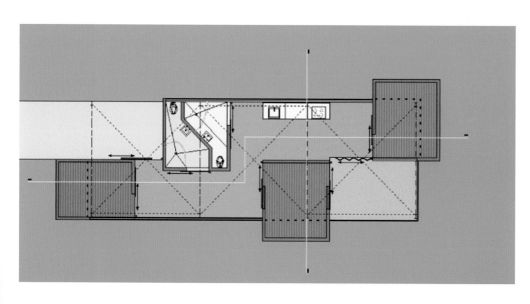

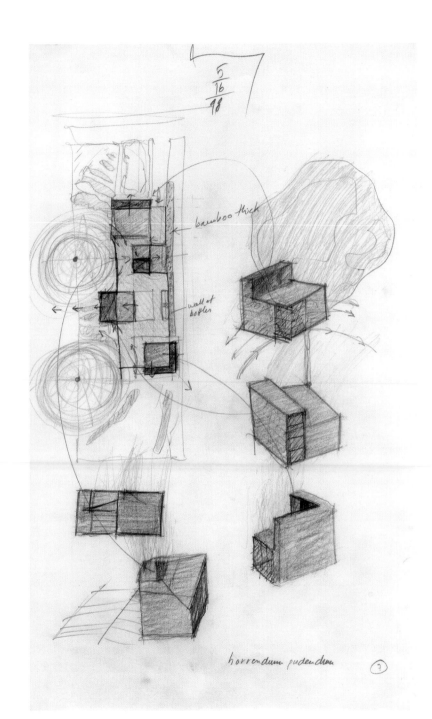

5
16
98

bamboo thick

wall of
boftles

horrendum pudendum

⑦

HOUSE IN HOUSTON
VOUCHER

$\frac{5}{17}$
$\frac{}{98}$

ZOHEMIC
CANOPY

H_2O

pump

energy flows
propensity

Gardens are made and shaped by people. For cultivation, leisure, and play, we arrange the ground around us to reflect our place and time. Designing a garden for someone else implies that one is aware of the client's needs, hopes, and desires. This is not the case with most low-cost housing in America. The client is anonymous and class-defined, someone in need of shelter.

So how is a garden designed in this context? A good place to start is with the vernacular garden. Composed by the dweller, it is idiosyncratic and improvisational. Objects are purchased, made, and found. Over time the garden grows and changes to reflect the rhythm of the everyday and the mundane. Like a quilt, its pieces are held together with a simple structure that allows easy change and variation.

The garden of the low-cost house starts with a simple structure and objects. The structure is a natural line that flows from front to back. It is an indication of the movement of the occupant and of nature; it changes with the structural alteration of the building. In this project, the lines, constructed with open-face concrete block, await the building and garden additions. A planting bed composed of mulch meanders along the north side of the house, and two oak trees are planted along the south side. The trees are staggered; desire lines will produce a path. Two steel drums serve as cisterns, catching and storing rainwater for cultivation. In the backyard, vegetable plots are established with topsoil. The perimeter fence is chain-link. In time the occupant will add paths and plantings, a storage shed and various objects, and maybe a patio, changing the plants and objects according to the season.

—**Walter Hood (Hood Design)**

Ruggedly Riley rode the roiling rapids by riverine rock and reef and rush, regaling righteously at the rightful Right of those who would rashly rout the riverlife in rhythm with its run. Riley's rhapsodic river rundown rubbed the roaring riptide wrongly, ripping roof and rudder and rundle from the royally rotten rest, wreaking riot, ruin, and remorse from poor rake Riley. Ruffled and reeling beyond rescue or reprieve, Riley ranged and rambled and railed, wretchedly wrestled right from wrong while raging relentlessly at the ruthless rule of the riverrun. Ruggedly Riley rode the roiling rapids by riverine rock and reef and rush, regaling righteously at the rightful Right of those who would rashly rout the riverlife in rhythm with its run. Riley's rhapsodic river rundown rubbed the roaring riptide wrongly, ripping roof and rudder and rundle from the royally rotten rest, wreaking riot, ruin, and remorse from poor rake Riley. Ruffled and reeling beyond rescue or reprieve, Riley ranged and rambled and railed, wretchedly wrestled right from wrong while raging relentlessly at the ruthless rule of the riverrun. Ruggedly Riley rode the roiling rapids by riverine rock and reef and rush, regaling righteously at the rightful Right of those who would rashly rout the riverlife in rhythm with its run. Riley's rhapsodic river rundown rubbed the roaring riptide wrongly, ripping roof and rudder and rundle from the royally rotten rest, wreaking riot, ruin, and remorse from poor rake Riley. Ruffled and reeling beyond rescue or reprieve, Riley ranged and rambled and railed, wretchedly wrestled right from wrong while raging relentlessly at the ruthless rule of the riverrun.

—**Sanford Kwinter**

Rugg	the roiling rapids pas
rush,	ously at the rightful I
rout	rhythm with its run. Y
rundown rubbed the	roaring riptide wrong
rundle from the royally rotten rest, wreak
from roughneck Riley and the less than re
beyond reprieve, rescue or repair, Riley ra
wretchedly wrestled right from wrong whi
raging the ruthless rule of riverrun Rugge

12 - 4 - 1 - 6 1/4" = 1'-0"

	the roiling rapids past r
	ously at the rightful Rig
	rhythm with its run. Yet
rundown rubbed the roaring riptide wrongly,
rundle from the royally rotten rest, wreaking
from roughneck Riley and the less than relia
beyond reprieve, rescue or repair, Riley range
wretchedly wrestled right from wrong while
raging the ruthless rule of riverrun Ruggesd

3 2 - 1 1/2" = 1'-0"

—**Bruce Mau**

This project transforms the fit and finish of a traditional house, loosening joints and treating walls as curtains that form a backdrop for everyday objects. It allows the house to breathe by peeling away the skin. Surfaces are used to differentiate various zones within the house (cooking, sleeping, eating). The homeowner can buy off-the-shelf components and products according to his or her particular tastes or needs, and these components can be switched as a family's desires and requirements evolve.

In his essay "What's So Funny: Modern Jokes and Modern Architecture," Brian Boigon notes, "Ed Sullivan liked the vaudeville version of his curtain to be tight up against him. Ed's producers kept his candid personality in the foreground by blending Ed's suit with the curtain itself. I could suggest that Ed was just one big curtain—one big surface—no outside inside, just Big Daddy bringing home the toys for the whole family . . . Johnny Carson's curtain was set quite far back from the front of the camera/stage. His set-up gave the impression that television was the stage of live truth. Carson gave the curtain wall a new spatial presence that empowered the foreground to erase the background . . ."

Ed Sullivan became his curtain; Johnny Carson broke from his. These transformations liberated both men from their sets. The depth of space and the continuity of surface allow the stuff of the house, and in the house, to exist as stuff.

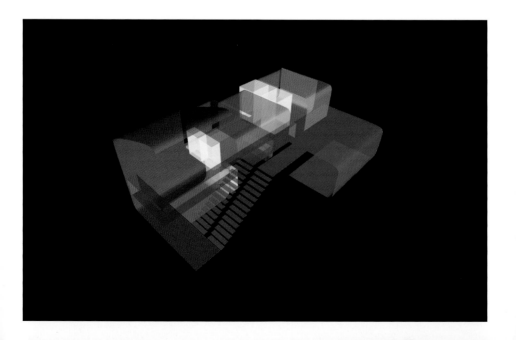

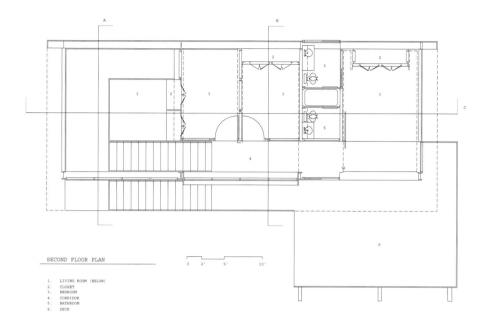

SECOND FLOOR PLAN

	0 2' 5' 10'

1. LIVING ROOM (BELOW)
2. CLOSET
3. BEDROOM
4. CORRIDOR
5. BATHROOM
6. DECK

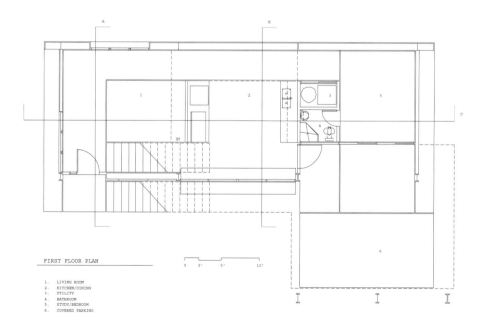

FIRST FLOOR PLAN

	0 2' 5' 10'

1. LIVING ROOM
2. KITCHEN/DINING
3. UTILITY
4. BATHROOM
5. STUDY/BEDROOM
6. COVERED PARKING

Three different lifestyles—extended family, squatter, and executive couple—served as case studies in the development of Klip, a consumer-based housing platform. Klip provides the physical and operational infrastructure—the binding device—that joins interchangeable units manufactured by various corporations to meet the needs of modern lifestyles. In the Klip system, occupants either buy or lease components from the corporations. The components offer a variety of options and upgrades; they are assembled with the Klip Binder, an adjustable joining mechanism. All components are take-home and Klip-compatible.

Services such as maintenance, exchange, upgrades, and returns are provided by local Klip dealers or home-shopping outlets. Satisfaction is guaranteed. Just as a television set or an automobile might be traded in, the Klip system responds to changing housing needs with twenty-four-hour service, on-line trade-in options, and a money-back guarantee. All options are available without real-estate fees, lending regulations, and the anxieties associated with conventional housing industries.

Alternative housing strategies exist.

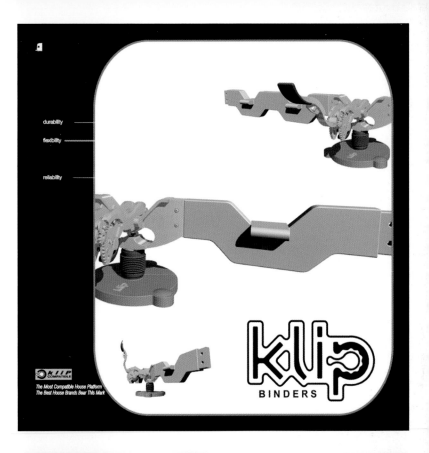

durability ————

flexibility ————

reliability ————

The Most Compatible House Platform
The Best House Brands Bear This Mark

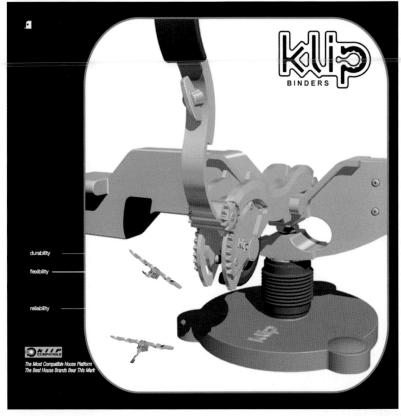

durability ————

flexibility ————

reliability ————

The Most Compatible House Platform
The Best House Brands Bear This Mark

KLIP BINDERS
1420 Sul Ross No. 2
HOUSTON, TX 77006
www.kliphouse.com

DATE	06 / 27 / 01
INVOICE NO.	0000728
TRANSACTION NO.	#000147
EMPLOYEE	Kenseth 0017

CUSTOMER INFORMATION

The Extended Family
123 Dover Lane
Houston, TX 77226-3307
(713)989-3333 (713)989-7000

PRODUCT INFORMATION

BINDER LICENSE NO.	**0000728**
ASSEMBLY CONFIGURATION	**Single Rail**
UTILITY CODE	**5**
VOUCHER NO.	**US 46589348-9903-77226TX**

ITEM NO.	BRAND / COMPONENT		SIZE	QTY.	TYPE	SPEC.
2397-2 nf	North Face	sleepklip	6' x 15'	1	leased	
8798-1 tr	Therma-rest	sleepklip	6' x 15'	1	purchased	
0597-4 ps	PlaySkool	babystation	3' x 12'	1	leased	pink
4829-1 ac	Academy	kidklip	6' x 12'	1	leased	translucent fill
4867-4 ac	Academy	kidSleep	3' x 9'	1	leased	
0592-4 ps	PlaySkool	fuzzyklip	3' x 9'	1	leased	lime
0278-3 ma	Mattel	playport	6' x 12'	1	leased	extension req.
0275-1 ma	Mattel	light-extension	6' x 3'	1	leased	port required
3339-6 mb	Mobil	h2o heater	3' x 9'	1	leased	
8765-2 om	Office Max	store-space	3' x9'	2	lease	
2446-2 rm	Rubbermaid Closet	klip	3' x 9'	1	purchased	
3864-4 uh	U-Haul	Space Saver	6' x 12'	1	purchased	
8909-5 ke	Kenmore	airChiller	3' x 9'	2	lease	
8956-5 ke	Kenmore	Washklip	6' x 9'	1	lease	
2278-8 co	Coleman	Cooker	3' x 9'	1	purchased	
2475-3 rm	Rubbermaid	Swingklip set	6' x 9'/6' x 12'	1	leased	
0075-5 rm	Rubbermaid	Swing step		2	leased	trim
0394-2 ig	Igloo	Chillklip	3' x 12'	1	leased	
2369-1 oz/wh	Ozarka/Whirlpool	deluxeklip	6' x 12'	1	purchased	
6640-6 bf	BFI	fullport	6' x 12'	1	leased	bfi blue
6647-3 bf	BFI	halfport	6' x 12'	1	leased	translucent
2475-3 rm	Rubbermaid	Kitnette	6' x 12'	1	leased	extension req.
0075-4 rm	Rubbermaid	light-extension	6' x 6'	1	leased	port required
2449-8 co	Coleman	Cookerklip	3' x 9'	1	purchased	red
0867-2 se	John Deere	toolPort	6' x 9'	1	purchased	dual lock
3867-2 uh	U-haul	freeklip	6' x 15'	1	leased	
6440-3 bb	Best Buy	systemklip	6' x 12'	1	leased	
0098-7 zi/dc	Zippo/ Duracell	fire/powerport	3' x 12'	1	leased	
2467-3 rm/ml	Rubbermaid/Maglite	entryklip	6' x 12'	1	purchased	
8765-2 om	Office Max	taskklip	6' x9'	1	leased	
0698-0 nk	Nike	hoopShoot		1	purchased	
0997-4 ml	Maglite	yardBright		3	leased	surface mount

PRODUCT UPDATE / ANNOUNCEMENTS

Call for an upgrade on your
Sony Surroundklip #3498-SO-3 and receive
a 25îscreen klip with surround sound - absolutely free.

Your house is next. **SONY**

MONTHLY TOTAL

STATE LEASE TAX

STANDARD PAYMENT

X
_____
Authorized & Received By

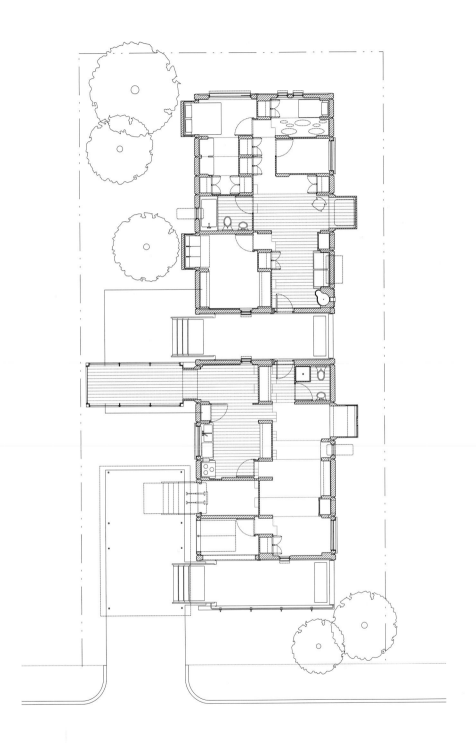

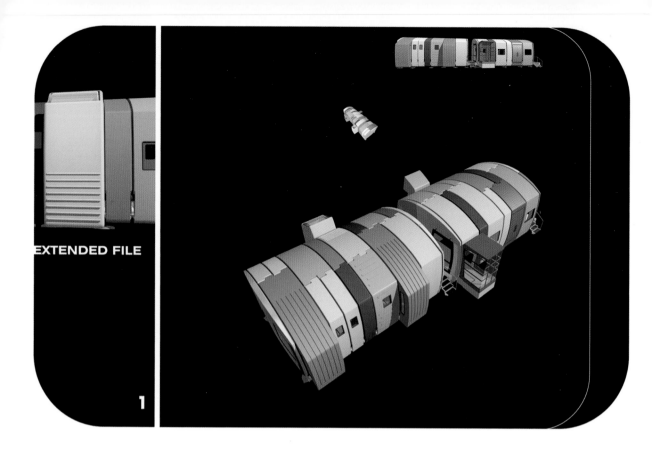

EXTENDED FILE

1

136

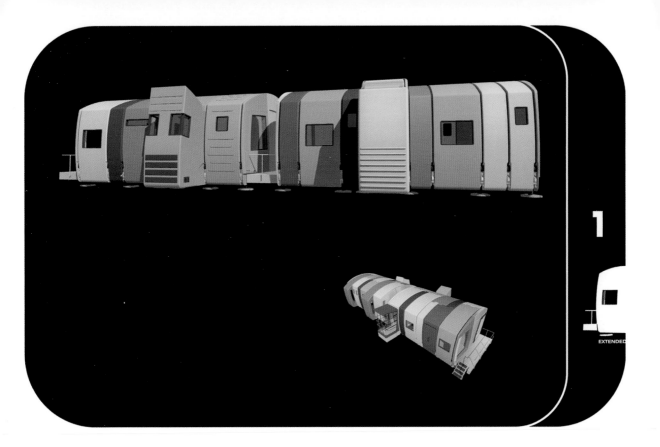

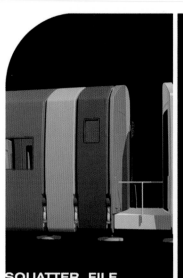

SQUATTER FILE

2

EXECUTIVE FILE

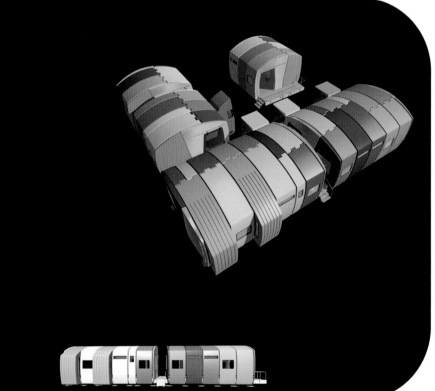

3

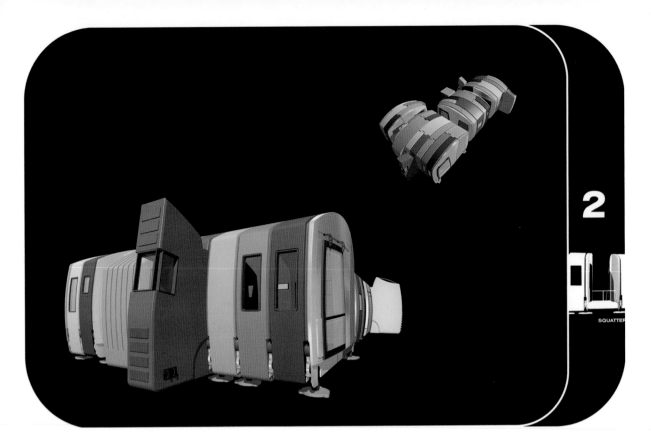
SQUATTER

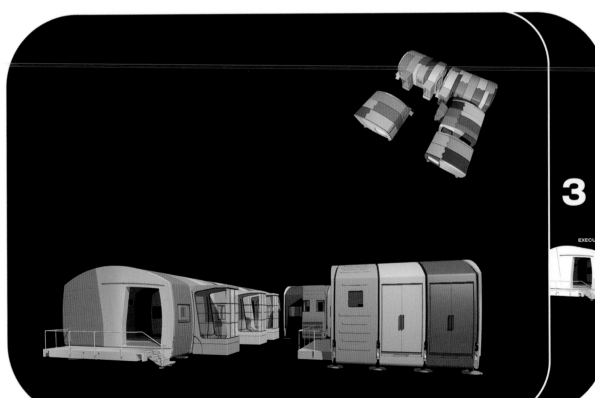
EXECUTIVE

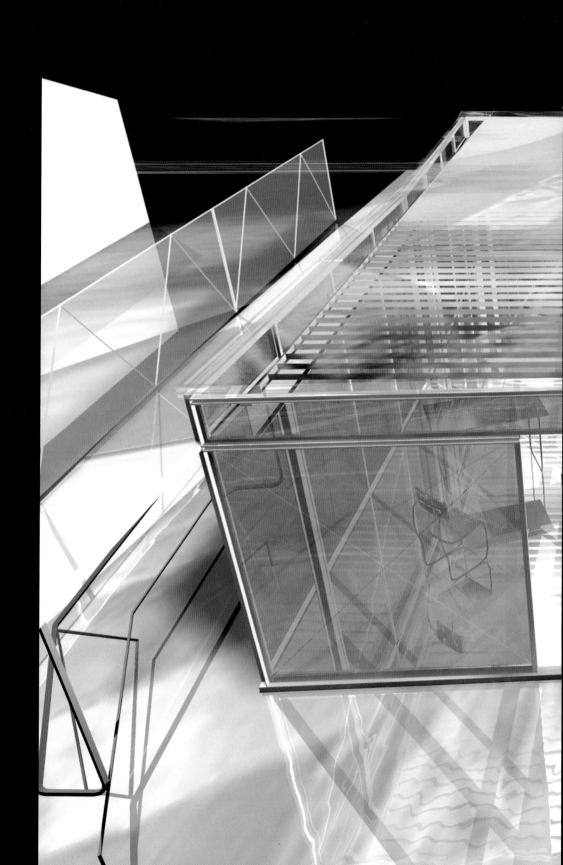

GLASS HOUSE @ 2 DEGREES **MICHAEL BELL**

PROJECT TEAM: JOHN MUELLER, TODD VAN VARICK; SPECIAL THANKS TO JOSHUA TEAS

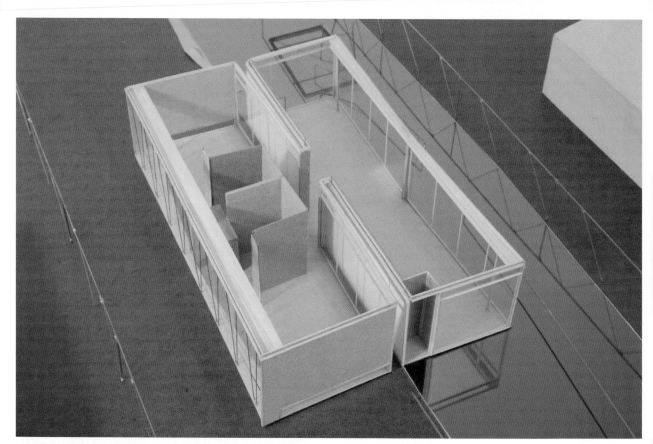

142

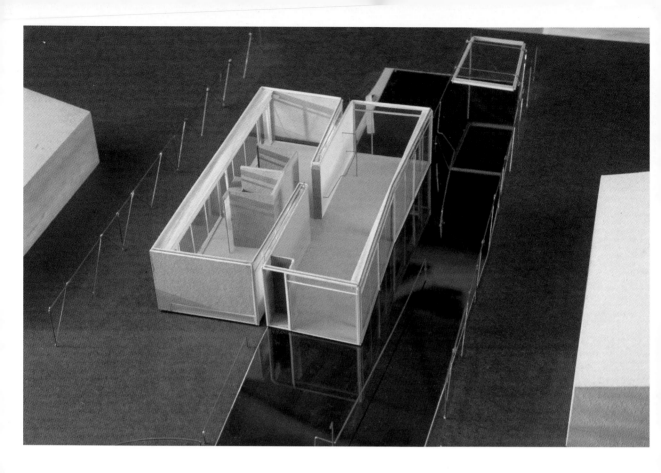

This nine-hundred-square-foot, two-bedroom, two-bath house sits on a mid-block site. The living spaces face north to a courtyard. The basic building component is a premanufactured sliding-door system. The twenty-four-by-forty-foot building is enclosed by four twenty-foot-long sliding-door panels. The panels are insulated glass, and the frames have a thermal break to provide energy efficiency. The house can be expanded to eleven hundred square feet to create a third bedroom. The foundation, concrete slab on grade, is finished with a resilient resin-based poured surface. The roof system is metal decking with rigid insulation and a polyurethane membrane. A light-gauge steel frame supports the roof. The bathroom and bedroom walls are made of folded metal backed with rigid sound insulation.

The alternate inside-outside panels of the glass doors slide along a planar center of gravity and alter the rotational momentum of the balanced track. The building folds in on itself to form two shallow light wells that bounce light into the bedrooms. The two-degree fold results from a push at each corner of the building; the north and south elevations appear to implode at the center. Glass House @ 2 Degrees is a plate structure—the taut surfaces of the tempered glass reveal tensions and energies.

The house is an approximation of a continuous surface, a folded structure with a topology determined by the dimensions of mass-produced components. The form is a working compromise between philosophy, mathematics, geometry, and production. It is a lens that affords a new view of the city and reveals a tentative, complex, yet powerful grasp on an elusive life. In Houston's Fifth Ward, the strife of income, race, class, geography, and movement or flight is raging, even as it is held in the static grip of silent governance. Glass House @ 2 Degrees is a monument to this moment.

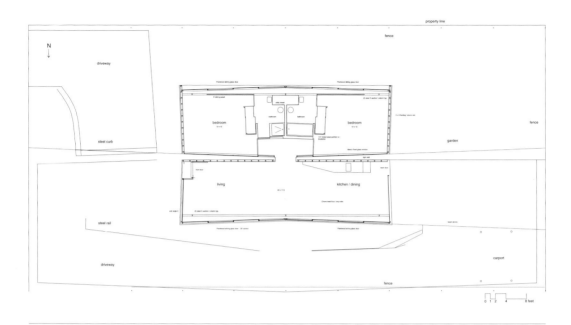

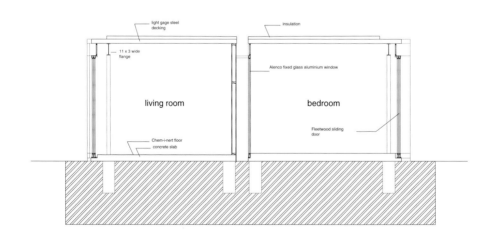

Variable House is not a single house but a strategy of ownership achieved through the configuration of space. Owning a house is more than owning land, materials, fixtures, and appliances. Ownership can be expressed by the process of creating a house, by the structuring of individualized space.

Because all families are unique, the space they inhabit should also be unique: the mechanisms, functions, and dimensions of the house should accommodate the dynamics of the occupants; the occupants should not limit themselves to the physical restrictions of the house. Variable House can be configured by its inhabitants—with the selection of design modules and materials—into various houses that each respond to particular living patterns. The house becomes characteristic of its owners as family sizes change, the necessity to work at home arises, the need for privacy or openness alternates, or the flexibility to accommodate unforeseen uses is required.

To expand the perceived size of the modest lived space and owned territory, Variable House offers openness with the immediate relationships it creates between interior and exterior spaces: a large living area connects directly to a garden; wide porches foster interactions with the neighborhood; expansive windows align with sunlight paths and cross breezes, permitting light and ventilation while reducing energy costs. Components, dimensions, and modules are standardized to achieve economy and efficiency in design and construction yet allow for the maximum variability of space, the maximum sense of ownership.

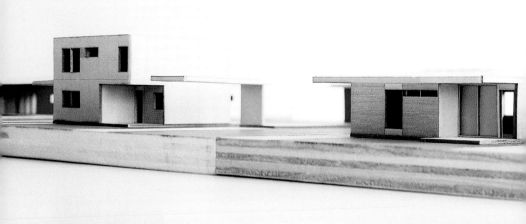

One and a Half House

Merge House

Twist House

Between House

Notch House

Ample House, first floor

Ample House, second floor

Flip House

Float House

Wrap House

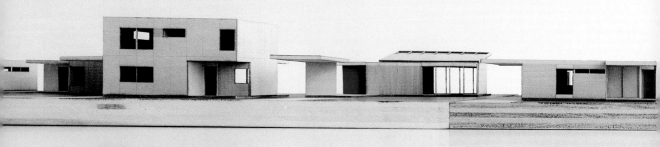

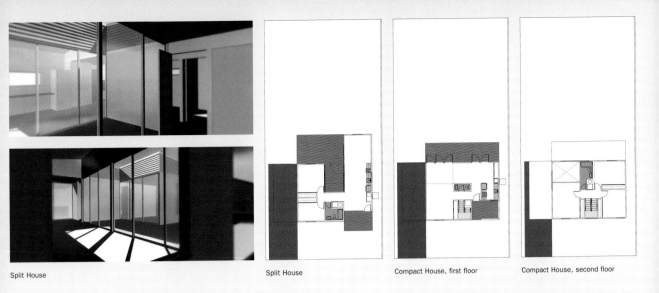

Split House

Split House

Compact House, first floor

Compact House, second floor

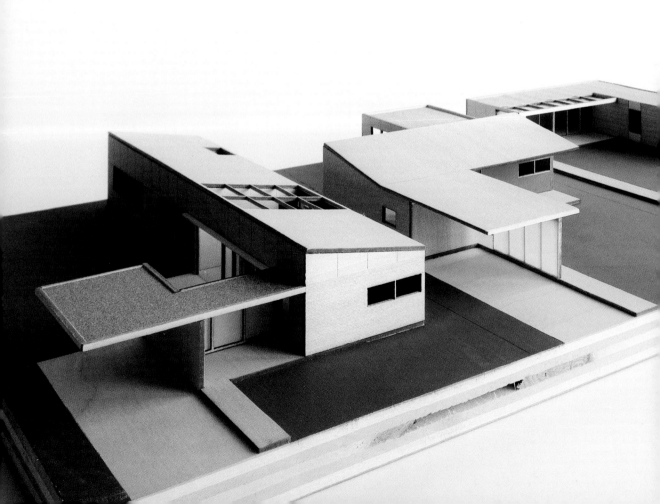

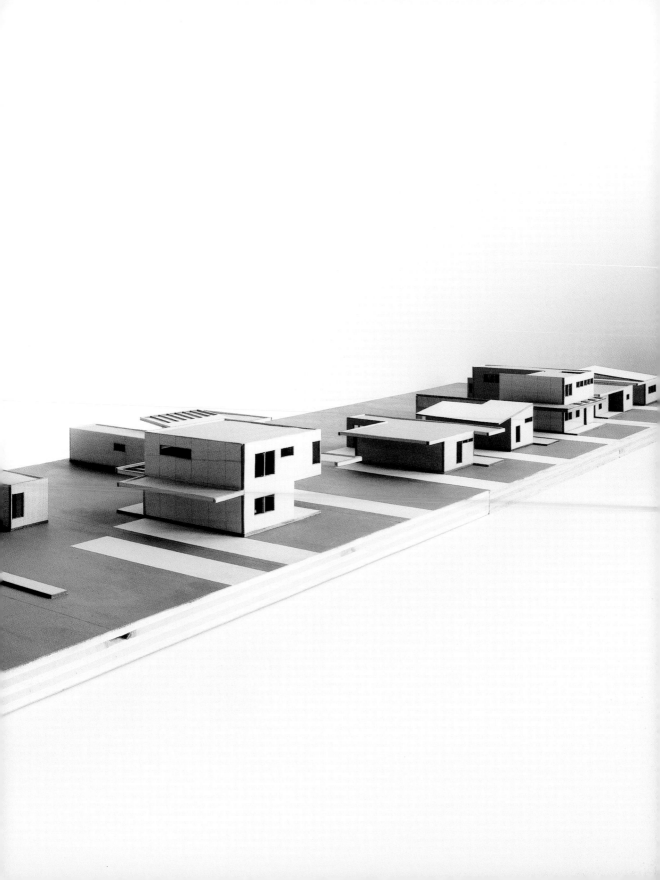

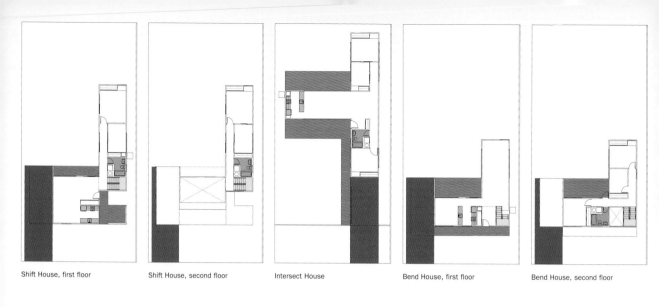

Shift House, first floor   Shift House, second floor   Intersect House   Bend House, first floor   Bend House, second floor

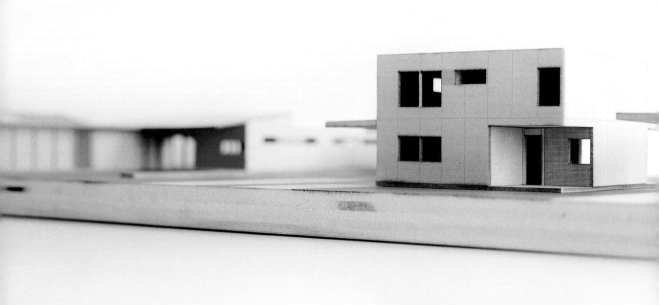

Stretch House

Stretch House

Split House (extended)

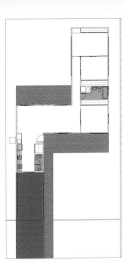

Spread House

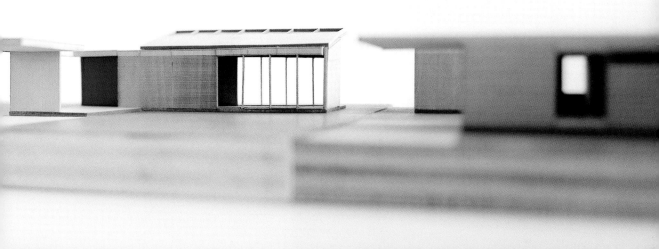

In Context

Before 16 Houses Was 16 Houses

Emily Todd Executive Director, DiverseWorks Artspace (1995–99)

One afternoon in August 1997, I met Michael Bell for lunch at a restaurant located in a former ballet supply store. As he told me of his research into the costs of housing development, I quailed: the preference for short-term profits over long-term investment struck my conservationist heart as wasteful; I railed against the lack of foresight shown by our community. Bell continued, describing the aesthetic shortcomings of this sort of development, and mused about how to get more architects involved in designing these structures to redress the current situation.

I was drawn to the research Michael was discussing. Was there an alternative to the bleak picture he painted? I was interested in stirring up a conversation about the issue and was prepared to involve DiverseWorks because of the ambitions of the project—a sort of David-and-Goliath scenario, in which Goliath was the powerful and omnivorous development community and *16 Houses* was the agile and canny David, representing the ability of the individual to question and confront. It seemed, at first, an improbable collaboration: DiverseWorks Artspace, with its reputation for cutting-edge, sometimes outrageous art, the architectural community, and the Fifth Ward Community Redevelopment Corporation seemed like three divergent entities, but there proved to be common ground in the idea of creating quality low-cost housing in the inner city. It was the belief in the power of the individual—in this case, homeowners, architects, and artists—that united these unlikely partners.

DiverseWorks is accustomed to complexity and experienced in offering possibilities. There is no question that *16 Houses* fit well within our mission: to be a place where artists could test new ideas in the public arena. This mission is deliberately flexible, intended to extend the nonprofit arts organization's reach into new territory as necessitated by artists' explorations. Since the organization's founding in 1983, its exhibitions and performances have actively explored artistic, cultural, and social issues. These public presentations showcase current (and often nonmainstream) ideas with the intent of inspiring a creative dialogue and building, educating, and sustaining audiences for contemporary art. At the core of DiverseWorks's mission is the belief that the work that happens there can effect change, even if only in one person at a time, and that perhaps the exploration demonstrated within its walls can be replicated outside. DiverseWorks's raison d'etre is to provide a crucible for experimentation and a pulpit for those whose ideas might not otherwise be shared.

As for myself, I wanted to work with architects for many reasons. The daughter of an architecture professor, I grew up in a great house, surrounded by conversations about the power of architecture. Having had this experience, I am convinced that space affects its inhabitants, and that well-designed space allows for wondrous possibilities. It follows that I believe the converse: that poorly designed space is damaging.

Moreover, architecture is often left out of the gallery context. Architects have long supported the arts in Houston with relatively little corresponding attention. DiverseWorks had a history with inner city and urban planning issues, and *16 Houses* had the potential to influence the way people in Houston talked about architecture and about our city. It would tackle the topic of affordable, architect-designed housing in the inner city and target an often-neglected audience: low-income individuals who generally do not have a say in architectural decisions. The exhibition presented the possibility that people who had never owned a house could reside in a special space, an individual space, ambitiously designed and affordably built. I was drawn by this marriage of values, theory, and practice. The exhibition gave DiverseWorks the opportunity to participate in the ongoing reinvestment in Houston's Fifth Ward neighborhood. The residents and the neighborhood were in the foreground in a positive light.

The context within which the house designs were presented helped to fuel the process. DiverseWorks was able to lend considerable expertise to the arrangement, design, and installation of the exhibition. Placing *16 Houses* in this environment imparted a different aura to the show than it would have had if presented at, say, City Hall, a community center, a builders' association convention, or even a university gallery.

During the installation of the exhibition, the gallery took on the character of a neighborhood coming to life: each display structure represented bare lots becoming construction sites. The models were presented simply and uniformly, in a grid formation reminiscent of city blocks. Moving through the gallery from model to model was not unlike taking a walk around a block. The models carried signs of life—from cars parked in driveways to well-kept gardens—and elicited speculation about the histories that would be set into motion once the houses were built.

16 Houses was not the promotion of sixteen solutions, but rather the fostering of a dialogue. The exhibition contained bold and thoughtful statements by people who believe their work can make the world better. Or at least this is my interpretation. It is certainly my belief that architecture has the transformative power of art. Good work makes the world better by countering mass production and mass consumption. This notion, coupled with a love of experimentation, adventure, creativity, and beauty, led to DiverseWorks's participation in the project. The project felt right personally, and it felt right institutionally.

It is impossible to convey the energy, the almost messianic conviction that animated and sustained this complex endeavor. The time was right and everyone proceeded despite the many and various obstacles that sprang up over the months. Ambition, optimism, and the potential for an improved social and aesthetic landscape galvanized the collaborators, while the opportunity to design, exhibit, and possibly build the projects invigorated the architects and artists.

16 Houses: Owning a House in the City helped to confirm the power of DiverseWorks's mission, and demonstrated the strength of a unique collaboration between three different groups of people. DiverseWorks was able to catalyze interaction between architects, artists, and their audiences, and to serve as an arena for a broad range of ideas and projects that might otherwise not have had an avenue for expression or realization.

No Place Like Home

Mardie Oakes Project Manager, Fifth Ward Community Redevelopment Corporation
(1995–2000)

Lawrence "Lucky" Evans was a man I am grateful to have known. He was the proud owner
of a new FWCRC two-story house in the heart of the neighborhood. Born and raised in the
Fifth Ward, he worked at the C & L Shoe Shop on Lyons Avenue for as long as many can
remember, save his time in Vietnam. I loved the long wall of elevated shoe-shine chairs, the
pungent smell of polish, the ever-present tapping of the hammer, and watching him resole
old cowboy boots or alligator dress shoes. It would always take a moment for my eyes to
adjust to the low light and, when they did, Lucky would be smiling.

I began working at the FWCRC in 1996, getting a crash course in inner-city development.
Despite a background in architecture, I was unprepared for the complexity of challenges
involved in getting projects built, especially because of the limits in funding and human
resources. I learned quickly that people, more often than not, emphasize what cannot be
done—obstacles ranging from the big picture of neighborhood revitalization to the pulling of
a single water permit. I learned almost as quickly not to listen to them; the vision of something better must pull you through. I also learned that because the FWCRC was a small organization, each of us needed to do a little bit of everything. Along with managing commercial
development projects, I was responsible for acquiring land for new single-family houses. This
required hours of driving the streets of the Fifth Ward, looking for vacant lots, especially where
the grass had been cut a couple of months before. If it had been longer ago than that, it was
likely the owner would be hard to find; if it had been cut more recently, the owner probably
had distant hopes of building there himself someday. It was this part of the job that allowed
me to immerse myself in the fabric and the people of the neighborhood. On good days I would
happen upon one of our homeowners working in his or her yard, excited about the responsi-
bilities that came with the new house. The FWCRC also brought new people into the neighborhood. Our prospective homeowners were like permanent fixtures at the office: they came
in to check on the progress, wondering which holiday would be their first in the new house, or
to bring another document required by the bank, or just to say hello. Whenever the foundation for a house was poured, we always got a panicked visit: even in large houses, the foundation looks so small before the walls go up.

Lucky was one of the homeowners who would pop in to say hello. He died of cancer in late
January 2000 at the young age of fifty-two, leaving behind several children and a wife with a
stunning name, Twynceola Batiste. I had the privilege of attending his funeral at the Pleasant
Hill Missionary Baptist Church. It was packed, a vast landscape of colored hats, and floral
wreaths on wire stands lined the stage, with ribbons grazing the floor. Many of the ribbons

had "Fifth Ward" printed on them in glitter. It seemed there was a preacher for every decade Lucky was alive, and many were friends that he used to "run" with as a child. They all got up and spoke about the Lucky they knew then and the Lucky they knew after he found God and the love of a good woman. One preacher's message: "Who else but God could let a shoe-shiner from the Fifth Ward drive a Cadillac? Who else but God could let a shoe-shiner live in a brand-new two-story home? And I ask you, who else but God could offer a shoe-shiner an even *smoother* ride, in a chariot drawn by white horses? Who else but God could offer an even *bigger* mansion in the great Heaven above?"

The program printed the following letter, as if Lucky were writing from the great beyond:

> *Dear Family and Friends:*
>
> *I want to let you know that I have moved. I received a call from God the Chief Architect who informed me that my new home is ready and that I could move in immediately. You all know that I have been sending up my timber, packing up getting ready to go, but there were some minor finishing touches on some of the timber that only the Chief Carpenter Jesus Christ could do. Some were a little too broad, thick, or not long enough.*
>
> *Well, my new home is finished and it's such a beautiful sight to behold. It is located in an exclusive estate area and it sits behind a beautiful Pearly Gate, just off a serene celestial shore. Of course, the streets are paved with gold and every day is Sunday here, I have been told. I lived in many places before my new home was prepared and none of the others can compare. There is peace, joy, and happiness here with no more pain to bear. No strife or discontent, there is only sweet serenity everywhere and I could go on about my new home, but I have to get fitted for my new robe.*
>
> *Let me give you my new address:*
> *Lawrence Evans*
> *52 Jesus Way*
> *Godstown, Heaven 3777*
>
> *P.S. I don't have a telephone yet, but just call. If you don't have the number, he's listed in the Good Book on every page.*

Is it a stretch to identify this service, this language, with a deeper, imbedded meaning about the importance of home? I don't think so. Many Fifth Ward residents place such importance on time spent at home with family and friends. Work is certainly valued too; there was a pair of pristinely shined alligator shoes carefully placed on Lucky's casket. But the home seems to hold a special meaning. Is it that many of the individuals who live in the Fifth Ward grew up there? Is it that a home of their own is something they never thought possible? Is it that owning a home means being one step closer to the elusive American dream? Is it that if they own their houses they can have some control over their surroundings? Is it the desire to pass something of value on to their children? I don't presume to have the answer, having heard many different families' particular reasons over the years. But I will say that I have witnessed a commitment to family and faith seven days a week, not just on Sunday, revealed in small details like answering machines that say "have a blessed day" before the beep.

The goal of the FWCRC is to do everything necessary to make a family's dream of home-ownership come true, from cleaning up credit to constructing the house. The mission of the FWCRC is to stabilize the Fifth Ward through homeownership, economic development, beau-tification, and neighborhood safety. There is no income maximum for the program, though subsidies are dependent on being below at least eighty percent of median income. A family making as little as twenty-seven percent of median income has been able to purchase a house through the program.

From the perspective of the FWCRC, this neighborhood will only thrive if its population is increased by not just low-income, but middle- and even high-income, residents. Neighborhood businesses rely on people with disposable income to survive, and neighbor-hoods stay viable by offering convenient amenities to their residents. If the FWCRC were to limit its clients to low-income residents, they would be doing the neighborhood a disservice. As the area gradually develops, the first low-income homeowners will reap the benefits of ris-ing property values, further increasing their equity. There are clear concerns about this process, but they can be ignored as long as the neighborhood continues to be marginalized by the greater Houston public. Clearly the threat of gentrification is ever-present. Neighborhoods that go from cold to hot too fast lose the very individuals that made them vibrant. If people rent and do not own, rising property values will result in higher rents, forc-ing them to move. And even for homeowners, a rapid increase in property taxes can be enough to make house payments difficult.

Long before the Fifth Ward faces these challenges, many immediate difficulties exist. Securing land is difficult at best. In a community where wills are uncommon or not record-ed, tracing ownership can be an arduous task. To purchase one five-thousand-square-foot lot for five thousand dollars took fourteen months and the securing of agreement and heirship affidavits from eleven different owners. The energy required on their part in order to pocket about $450 apiece made the process a tedious one at best.

Challenges specific to the *16 Houses* designs range from infrastructural to educational. The way mortgages are bundled and sold by banks to organizations like Fannie Mae requires houses to fall into neat and tidy categories (e.g., all Hardiplank exterior, three-bedroom, two-bath houses with a two-car garage go into one bundle). If the bank holds a house that does not fit nicely into a category, it may be stuck with a mortgage that is expensive to service on its own. Appraisers can only assign value to a feature that has been proven in the mar-ketplace. What this means is that until an individual or institution with equity to spare builds a house with polished concrete floors and sells it at a high value in the same general vicin-ity as the prospective new houses, the appraiser cannot give credit to polished concrete floors as a positive feature, and may even discount the value. This is why building prototypes is so critical to getting good work built in the future. The first ones are the hardest to sell—that is, assuming they do sell.

Architectural education of prospective home-buyers is critical and sorely lacking across all incomes. When I first came to work at the FWCRC, I noticed that families would rarely spend more than fifteen minutes selecting their floor plans. I spend longer than that choosing a pair of shoes. This is the house they intend to live in for at least five years, the minimum time required for second mortgages to convert into grants. Many intend to stay in their houses until they pass on to that mansion in the sky, yet they have no way to critically assess the plans or to understand how the house could fit into their lives or express their personalities. It is an architecturally undemanding market, which I believe can only be changed when people *experience* good buildings.

16 Houses was a powerful vehicle in this educational process. With the exhibition at DiverseWorks Artspace on the edge of the Fifth Ward providing scale models of each design that were accessible to those with no formal training in architecture, people began to get excited. What I realized is that many people's only experience of nontraditional architecture is through television and movies, the scene of some slick, twenty-thousand-square-foot estate overlooking the San Francisco Bay as a backdrop for an upscale party or an FBI raid. *16 Houses* allowed people to imagine themselves inside, living a life, raising a child, or throwing a party in a unique and creative environment at a price they could afford. Most important, it offered the possibility of choice, a luxury this population has been conditioned not to expect.

We have never pretended that these houses are the solution for the greater population. What we have seen is that there are families and individuals who want something different from what is usually offered, but they are hard to find until something like the *16 Houses* show comes along. After all, with developers dumbing down designs to meet the perceived needs of the largest market, this more discerning population is invisible. They do not have the opportunity to demonstrate their choice through the purchase of a house, as that choice is simply not available. *16 Houses* and the FWCRC hope to change that by building several of these designs. The obstacles have been many: inadequate city infrastructure supporting the site, a construction boom in Houston that increased costs at just the wrong time, an organization with limited resources taking the lead, some designs with bigger dreams than were financially feasible, and the impatience of home-buyers who wanted to start their new lives sooner rather than later. Still, the project moves forward, slowly but surely. I tell myself that if this were easy, it would have been done long ago.

The question remains, when all is said and done, will people want to live in these houses? Absolutely. Experiences like the one I had at the opening of a modernized historic row house in the heart of the Fifth Ward confirm that. I overheard an older woman from down the street say with a hint of skepticism, "I came because I heard there was a house without a ceiling." She stepped inside, saw the exposed rafters, ductwork, and decking and immediately realized how much larger the little house felt. She loved it. Had we tried to sell her a house with no ceiling on paper, it would not have happened. The construction and sale of a few of these houses will allow the Fifth Ward and greater Houston to take a step toward creating a built environment that enlivens our senses and transforms our vision of what a house can offer.

Negative Force

Albert Pope Gus Sessions Wortham Professor of Architecture, Rice University

Housing

The constant and indiscriminate use of the term "housing," a word that has continued importance to just about any definition of modern architecture, is on the verge rendering it meaningless. Such overuse obscures key concerns vital to the understanding of contemporary public housing and its early twentieth-century European predecessors, its intended occupants, and their relation to the city. Is there is a difference between a Bruno Taut housing block and a market-rate apartment house? When does a house become a unit of housing—a commodity—or more important, *why* does a house become a unit of housing? Must public housing necessarily be low-income? Must it be about standardization, *existence minimum*, economies of scale, and mass production? What defines housing as a distinct discourse and to what end is this discourse structured?

To answer some of these questions one only need imagine what the *16 Houses* exhibition would have been had it occurred fifty years earlier, in 1948 rather than 1998. For a start, the exhibition brief would have assumed the razing of five to ten blocks of the Fifth Ward, the demolition of most, if not all, of the through streets, and a substantial increase in urban density. Understood in this context, the solutions for an exhibition in 1948 are easy to imagine. Variations on the Ville Radieuse would have been proffered, along with a novel form of clustering and innovative unit plans. The Weissenhof settlement, Red Vienna, Bruno Taut, and Karl May would all have been mentioned. The Unité d'Habitation would only have been halfway through construction in Marseilles, but would already have been responsible for a raft of trickle-down. The immanent, geopolitical standoff between Hansaviertel Interbau and the Stalinallee in Berlin would have given a historic dimension to the proceedings. As the centerpiece of a newly arrived welfare state rising from the ashes of the last World War, housing was, in 1948, a heady political statement. It was an opportunity to do nothing less than represent, in a single, scrubbed superblock, the arrival of the modern city out of the ruinous indignities of a gridiron slum. For an entire generation of architects, it was the only game in town.

Much has changed since that moment, and there is no greater index of that change than the way housing is understood today. In 1948, housing was, by definition, an exercise in standardization. It was invariably proposed as high-density development combined with a generous amount of open space, and was often low-income—the economies of scale in fewer, larger buildings were thought to raise the housing standard for all. In 1998, housing is an exercise in customization. Following the presumed diversity of the clientele, houses are stylistically heterogeneous. They are proposed as low-density infill development combined with the revival of the pedestrian street and urban park. They are built not around economies of scale but around a considerable reinvestment in existing infrastructures, which brings the unit price down considerably.

The bridge that connects these two conceptions of housing is not short, and it seems unlikely that it could be spanned by a single word. If, on the other hand, these conceptions could be reconciled, it might indicate that something deeper links these opposed modes of urban intervention. "Housing" might be understood not as an outdated, overused term but as an idea that transcends its many manifestations. What then connects housing circa 1948 with housing circa 1998 as they both relate to America's embattled inner city?

Operative Scale

Postwar housing was realized not under the enlightened patronage of a welfare state but during the extravagant excess of postwar prosperity and the rise of consumerist values. Such a context accelerated the flight into the suburbs for all who could afford it and created an urban crisis of unprecedented proportions. The words "blight," "slum," and "ghetto" began to figure prominently in urban discourse at this time. It was also at this time that the inner city, as we now understand it, came into existence, casting a long shadow on all of the city it defined, including the Fifth Ward. Fifty years later, that shadow still exists. It has remained an intractable problem.

The solution of high-density towers and an excess of open space would not stay in favor for long in U.S. cities. It was for only a short moment—between the Housing Act of 1949 and the first demolitions of Pruitt-Igoe[1] in 1972—that planners, architects, politicians, advocacy groups, and their imagined users all came to believe that the modern city was our urban destiny, but the faith that drove this belief was absolute, at least up to the point at which twenty-three years of abject failure caught up with it.

In Europe and Asia, Radiant City planning fared much better. Despite similar setbacks, there has been no systematic destruction of modern blocks and slabs. On the contrary, over the past fifty years, large European and Asian cities have continued to build high-density settlements subject to the inexorable economic laws of economies of scale. As building has continued, typical settlements have grown from ten or fifteen midsize buildings to three or four very large buildings, usually tacked on to existing settlements. This development follows a trend of total interiorization, predicted thirty years ago, in the form of the megastructure or large housing settlements under a single roof.

Another fated prescription for North America, the megastructure had no more effect than Radiant City planning did. The laws concerning economies of scale have not, however, been suspended or reversed. Since 1948, the economies of scale operating in the United States have grown far larger than those in Europe. Instead of housing being accommodated in three or four large buildings, in the U.S. it is accommodated in thousands of very small buildings called tract houses. The North American corporate subdivision, planned as a single unit, has become the most pervasive of all megastructures and is rapidly expanding in size as it is being exported as a global phenomenon.

Such megastructures are rarely understood as such, yet their qualities are undeniable. For example, there are four primary subdivision-megastructures surrounding Houston, each approaching a population of one hundred thousand. They are all called "planned communities," and more than half of all new housing starts in Houston occur in one or another of them. They are conceived as a single entity, designed as a single entity by a single civil engineer, developed as a single entity, and administered as a single entity by a homeowner association. It is irrelevant whether the unit is small or detached or painted blue or gray. It is also irrelevant that it is widely dispersed. The tract may be spread over a large area, but its basic organization is still totalizing: with its hierarchical organization of streets, its strict, single-use zoning and closed, cul-de-sac planning, it is a megastructure in everything but name. It now dwarfs the environments from which it took its stylistic cues: the old, prewar gridiron suburbs, of which the Fifth Ward is an excellent example.

What Is a Slum: 1948?

The slum of 1948 is a non-city. It is the absence of city, or what the city becomes when urban energies fail. It is a pitiless, astral place profoundly marked by the lack of a collected presence. If there is collected presence, it exists only as a form of nostalgia for a socially, economically, and politically outmoded world. The gridiron slum is characterized by a rampant dereliction and, ultimately, the proliferation of open spaces that move in to replace the city. The slum is where the corridor street becomes something shameful and gridiron planning becomes mechanical and inhumane. There is no way to distinguish between the collapse of the inner city—whether the south Bronx, Detroit, or the south side of Chicago—and the collapse of the social world itself. The 1948 slum is where the city became a victim of circumstances, the toxic side effect of so much wrenching change. Such change is the reality in which modern architecture was born.

What Is a Slum: 1998?

The slum of 1998 is a non-city. It is Levittown writ large, mile after mile, tract after tract. It is an aerial view of fields, endless fields of production housing. It is the mono-semantic world where the tract house shows a limited variation and an infinite replication as it proudly presents to the street a blind garage door. Unlike the dilapidated cores of the inner city, today's slum is the result of an excess, rather than an absence, of planning. It is not the result of social catastrophe, new economic dispensations, or protracted warfare. It is not a victim of circumstance; it was, instead, thoroughly planned. It was always intended to be a closed system, achieved with the requisite cul-de-sac. It was always intended to depopulate and distend the city. It was always intended to eliminate the outward symbols of collective will. It was built to send a message, an indication that the city had realigned the necessary social, political, and economic forces correcting the failures that had plagued the nineteenth-century gridiron. It was the consequence of an elaborate proliferation of open space, of what continues to be called sprawl.

Nothingness by Design

What makes the contemporary subdivision so much more terrifying than the remnants of the burnt out inner cities is its intention. It was designed to be that way. As opposed to the inner cities that collapsed with the passing of an economic, social, or political order, the nothingness produced by the suburban slum is fully instrumental. The emptiness of the inner-city gridiron speaks of abandonment, dysfunction, and at the very best, a cold corporate largesse. The emptiness produced by the modern subdivision speaks of a preemptive planning that is so complete and encompassing as to eliminate the very prospect of reform.

Houston's Fifth Ward is apparently impervious to bureaucratic control. Fifty years of well-meaning intervention has failed to improve its lot. The post-urban subdivision, on the other hand, exhibits the very essence of bureaucratic control operating as it was always intended to operate. With the passing of so much time, and so much demolition and construction, can we now raise the possibility that the astral voids of the Fifth Ward are related to the astral voids of the exurban city? Are there not behind them both the same aspects of negation, the same disused pockets of space, the same obliteration of the urban foreground, the same stretches of asphalt, the same hostility to a pedestrian presence? Forget how unlikely it seems, could there not be behind them both a single motivating force? Perhaps the emptiness is not the effect of war, economic or political reversals, or the swift pace of technological change. Perhaps it is now willed to exist by design.

Reproducing Null Space

As redevelopment worked its way across the urban landscape, the open gridiron city was systematically written over by the closed planning of the Ville Radieuse slab and the closed cul-de-sac subdivision. From our present vantage, what seems most shocking is that it has become difficult to distinguish the old vacuous slum from the new vacuous slum. From void to void again, contemporary urban form seems less like redevelopment and more like a reproduction of the existential malaise it sought to replace. The similarity between the emptied gridiron of the Fifth Ward and the emptied cordon sanitaire, parking lots, and flood-control easements in and around the typical postwar suburb is obvious to see. They are both the spatial consequence of an apparent collapse of collected presence. Such presence is the beginning and the end of the city. Beyond it, what was considered the city simply does not exist anymore.

Instead of asking why we build environments so contrary to our collective nature, we might well ask what alternative we ever really had. In light of the twentieth century's revue of toxic ideologies pressed into the service of base and brutal ends, there was no real way, as the century proceeded, to reconstitute the urban project with any credible, coherent constituency. After the Second World War, the hopelessly utopian ambition of modernist practitioners to give form and meaning to mass society was rejected outright along with the Ville Radieuse. (It can be argued that the Ville Radieuse had intended to smuggle it into American cities, Trojan Horse–like, secretly hidden by so much welcome greenery.) The mass as an empowered spatial presence embedded in urban form stood zero chance of happening, regardless of how beautifully we designed our slabs and towers, our megastructures and retro-monuments.

In 1948 the welfare state had already begun to see its mission as the enfranchisement of a disinherited urban class. It was hoped that such a goal would restore collective meanings and pass them on as civilizing influences. Beyond this, however, there was little option but to peacefully deprogram urban space and reproduce the existential void that one might have understood, after the greatest of wars, as a necessary corollary to civil life. After the global atrocities committed under the cover of a collective will, civil life required, perhaps even welcomed, a vacuum. The ability to grasp such a vacuum as an ideological free zone (not to occupy it socially or turn it into a themed environment) is evident in the cities we have made ever since. This can be seen in the creation of the inner city (the not-so-peaceful deprogramming of civic life) as well as the creation of the closed urban systems that surround it.[2]

16 Houses

Here, finally, one can establish a context for the *16 Houses* exhibition and for the possibilities inherent in the inner city today. Still dazed and confused by the catastrophe of Pruitt-Igoe and the hundreds of slum-clearance projects that followed, we are seemingly only capable of promoting urban visions that are a pitiable infill into the nineteenth-century gridiron—the gridiron being the last city that we understood as such, and the last dimension of public life that deserved the name. These infill strategies rely on the ballast of nineteenth-century planning to sustain their meaning. As gridded infrastructures have not been built or extended in the past fifty years, infill strategies are, at best, a rearguard action. The existing nineteenth-century urban cores are now understood as a fixed commodity—one that is suffering the dual stresses of gentrification and dereliction—and we can only look forward to diminishing returns in the near future. Most important, however, infill strategies may delay the inevitable reckoning with twentieth-century models, specifically models that answer the legitimate needs now met by the European slab city and the American housing tract.

In spite of all this, when we turn to the Fifth Ward today what becomes clear, especially in light of the projects in this exhibition, is that this inner-city neighborhood is far less of a slum than the corporate tracts that surround it. The Fifth Ward is one of the most beautiful residential districts in the city, which is all but obscured by the apparent poverty of the area. So offensive is this situation that it is callous to talk about beauty in the context of it. Yet it is this beauty that must be understood if the redevelopment of the Fifth Ward is to be successful. For if the Fifth Ward is gentrified into another insulated community filled with muted tract houses and dead streets, then what was worth saving in the first place will be lost. What will be lost is a century's worth of African American history written into the buildings and the streets. What will be lost is a century's worth of growth of wild vegetation that makes this most central of neighborhoods apparently rural. What will be lost is a relative openness in the many empty lots that play host to previously unimagined programs. These lots and the streets that link them remain, in fact, full of people—in marked contrast to the absence of outward signs of life in the corporate housing tract, the upscale office park, and the ubiquitous strip center.

What would a strategy of intervention look like today? A first response would be easy: new houses, good schools, banks, pharmacies, and grocery stores. But to address only these issues would be to sell the Fifth Ward short. Of equal importance to establishing an economic base and a viable infrastructure is confronting head-on the vexing problem of gentrification. For as soon as these material improvements take place, the real-estate market would make a dramatic upward swing, leading to a crass commercialization accomplished on the backs of those working for social change. Gentrification would undoubtedly arrive in the Fifth Ward under the heading of urban renewal. Such renewal has less to do with recovering something that was lost than recognizing the marketing opportunity built into new infill construction. Such marketing would substitute for community building a pleasant narrative of return, revitalization, and recovery: a pure nostalgia driven—as is most urban development today—by a theme. This thematic consolidation is not so far-fetched and would be played out in the Fifth Ward as follows: throw a cordon around new development with multiple street closings; build a model house that recalls great houses from the past (steeply pitched roofs, leaded glass windows, front porches, high ceilings, real fireplaces), and most important, change the name from the Fifth Ward to Colonial Oaks Meadow, so it could become "a new upscale development in the center of Old Houston, homes starting in the low $300,000s." As quickly as pleasantries turn into sophistries, thematic consolidation would be set to deliver a prepackaged identity, and the Fifth Ward as it is understood today would cease to exist, which would be like a murder.

What, then, can a one-thousand-square-foot infill house do to defeat rather than accelerate the forces of gentrification? This question is answered, in large part, by the *16 Houses* exhibition itself. Some of the architectural projects included in this book give a far better answer than a couple of paragraphs in an essay ever could. Issues to look out for include the imagined scope of the projects: Some of the houses understand that the inner city is no neutral construct and that the construct itself is a large part of the problem. In this regard, they work outside the construct by exercising an acute awareness of the larger metropolitan field, particularly its spatial and thematic qualities. Some of them also understand the value of infill, not as an opportunity for spatial consolidation, but as a provisional process that is ongoing. They acknowledge that the open space the Fifth Ward has acquired after more than fifty years of dereliction is a resource, and perhaps a seventeenth, eighteenth, or nineteenth house would simply propose the banking of empty lots. Finally, some of the projects understand the value of stylistic diversity—not as an opportunity to invent new grammar, but as a way to preempt thematic consolidation—while others buy in to such consolidation, and ignore rather than confront the problem of gentrification.

Those who work for social change in inner-city neighborhoods often rush to design solutions, for it is often a desperate situation, yet it is rare that these interventions work outside the inner-city box, evaluating and reflecting the larger metropolitan field. Any intervention must respond to the legitimate needs now met by the corporate housing tracts that surround the inner city.

Does this mean seeking virtues in Radiant City planning or reproducing the disused, null space of the suburban periphery? The short, polemical answer is yes, this is exactly what it means. Such space may be alienating to the point of misery, but we deeply need it, its openness, its lack of friction, and the absence of specificity that are all important upsides to alienation. In addition to refusing spatial consolidation, we need to refuse thematic consolidation, especially when such consolidation is only a cynical marketing tool. In the end, who would not prefer an abundance of space to the claustrophobia of a wall-to-wall thematic development along the lines of Colonial Oaks Meadow?

More Questions

Is it possible to return to a time when housing was a moral imperative and the welfare state was a matter of conviction and faith? Is it possible to return to a time when housing was understood as "the problem of the epoch," when the unit became an empowering construct, and when the conception of the social world was confidently shared? The modern city as it was imagined fifty years ago has long passed into urban history, along with the welfare state that supported it, but it was once our destiny, and it might still be. If this is true, then our more recent excursions into the excesses of suburban sprawl will amount to nothing more than a half-century of stubborn denial.

Notes

1. Pruitt-Igoe was a massive ninety-eight-acre slum-clearance project in the center of St. Louis. When it opened in October 1954, it contained twenty-eight hundred units and approximately ten thousand occupants. The title of the April 1951 *Architectural Forum* article that first presented the built project speaks volumes: "Slum Surgery in St. Louis." In 1972, the first demolitions began. At that time, the vacancy rate was over 70 percent. Demolitions continued until 1976, when the last slab was imploded. Pruitt-Igoe is interesting in itself, but it is arguably more important as the first of such widespread demolitions, symbolic implosions of towers and slabs that were organized and cheered by the liberal politicians who commissioned them in the first place. It thus serves as a watershed in regard to modern city planning and its component slabs and towers. In hindsight, it is left for us to contemplate how a profound moment of social transformation became obscured by a tragically short attention span. In the end, what may be remarkable is not the fact that Pruitt-Igoe was destroyed so quickly, but that it ever existed at all.

2. I have argued elsewhere that such a species of free zone is the negative force that drives the global-urban environment today. See Albert Pope, *Ladders* (New York: Princeton Architectural Press, 1996).

More Design = Lesser Value

Michael Bell

During the winter of 1999, Mardie Oakes and I sought funding from the Local Initiatives Support Corporation of New York to help construct several of the sixteen houses. This money was granted to the FWCRC and resulted in the formation of a committee to select six architectural teams that would receive professional fees to complete contract documents. The committee selected seven projects, nominating the house by StudioWorks for special consideration. The other teams selected were Keith Krumwiede, Lindy Roy, Morris Gutierrez Architects, William Williams and Archie Pizzini, Carlos Jiménez Studio, and my own team.

The committee was composed of representatives from the Fifth Ward and the academic and architectural communities. Emily Todd, then-director of DiverseWorks Artspace, served as the chair. The committee included Reverend Harvey Clemons (president, FWCRC board of directors), Robert Toliver (builder and Fifth Ward resident), Stephen Fox (Anchorage Foundation), Farés El Dahdah (assistant professor, Rice University School of Architecture), Aaron Betsky (director, Netherlands Architecture Institute), and Jeff Balloutine (vice president for community reinvestment, Bank United).

During the spring and summer of 2000, the teams worked with the FWCRC, documenting the projects and verifying the affordability and practicality of construction. The Local Initiatives Support Corporation funding provided each team with consulting fees and also paid for the salary of a construction manager, who joined the staff at the FWCRC. Mardie Oakes and I acted as liaisons between the architects, the construction manager, and innovative subcontractors such as Metalab of Houston.

We also worked with Bank United of Houston to establish not only sales prices for the houses, but more important, projected appraisals for houses that had no economic or design precedent in the Fifth Ward. In most cases, the appraisals were lower than the sales prices, creating a deficit between the price of construction and the amount of funding available through mortgage financing. This situation is typical in low-income or impoverished areas, and it forced the FWCRC to serve two roles: that of developer, as anticipated, but also that of contractor. The FWCRC essentially eliminated profits from the construction process in an effort to deliver the project at a cost close or equal to its appraisal. Aggressive cost-cutting techniques made it possible for all seven houses to be built for a reasonable price, yet in each case the construction costs still exceeded the appraisal. The house by Carlos Jiménez came closest to balancing the cost and the appraisal, no doubt due to his experience in building lower-cost artists' housing in Houston.

We discovered that the more a project departed from traditional forms, the greater the disparity between the actual cost and the projected appraisals. It became clear that in the Fifth Ward, where there was already a suppressed valuation of property, nontraditional houses caused an even greater financial strain on the mortgage process. In short, low appraisals based on location were limiting the amount of design experimentation.

16 Houses began as an attempt to ascertain the value of design in lower-income market-rate housing. As a case study focused on the Fifth Ward and the merits of the voucher program, it revealed an expected but still startling suppression of innovation. It became evident that housing is not well served by market-based valuation practices.

Without functioning as both contractor and developer, the FWCRC would not have been able to overcome this obstacle or meet the mortgage guidelines that allowed the houses to be financed. Of course, these houses are also being constructed as onetime projects and do not have the cost advantage of mass production.

In 1989, when the FWCRC began its mission in the Fifth Ward, it faced similar difficulties with appraisals. There were no comparable houses in the Fifth Ward that could be used as a benchmark to value the newer yet essentially standard developer-type houses proposed. The FWCRC did not fear gentrification at that point, and the new houses were seen as a sign of economic revitalization. The FWCRC worked with a bank that was willing to establish a new and higher level of value despite the lack of comparable appraisals. Eleven years later, with *16 Houses,* the FWCRC again took extraordinary measures to build houses that had no precedent. In this case, the more traditional of the seven houses chosen by the committee provided a form of equity that balanced the less traditional houses.

For some, this balancing act may appear to be a compromise, but it ultimately reveals the degree to which the mortgage industry's efforts to preserve its capital and lower its risk limit design innovation. *16 Houses* tried to address this endemic, and virtually inevitable, condition by providing a graphic depiction of market values in relation to design and geography. The chart on the following page shows the sales price, appraisal value, and available mortgage funds for each of the seven houses. It does not reflect the voucher subsidy that would lower the sales price and, in effect, bridge the gap between mortgage and appraisal. That gap ranges from approximately $2,400 to $23,000.

At this writing, one of the projects has been completed: the house by Morris Gutierrez Architects began construction in December 2001 and is now occupied by owners who met voucher and FWCRC guidelines. Earlier that year, three other houses were under contract with buyers: the projects by Keith Krumwiede, Williams/Pizzini, and StudioWorks. They all successfully met construction costs, but again financial complications set in. The water main provisions for the three adjacent sites were substandard, and lengthy negotiations ensued between the City of Houston and the FWCRC over who should finance these services. The level of services provided by the city was below the standard common for every other community in Houston, and this kind of hurdle was typical. Two buyers withdrew from contracts after an eight-month delay; the third is still awaiting resolution of the negotiations.

The significance of each house might truly be the degree to which it offers even modest levels of innovation given the diminished valuations that all but preclude new construction in areas such as the Fifth Ward. While the Klip House and other projects offer new incentives for mass production—and thereby have the potential to improve the quality of housing—other works such as Lindy Roy's Vhouse and my own Glass House @ 2 Degrees use low-level craft, off-the-shelf parts, and typologically based forms. Like most of the houses, these two navigate between innovating and compromising with market forces, revealing an underlying skepticism about the viability of the voucher program and its ability to accomplish its stated goals. Unlike the housing exhibitions held in the 1940s and 1950s at the Museum of Modern Art, this exhibition reveals the relationship between the free market and the federal government, and the degree to which design and location act to either inspire or eliminate invention.

These sixteen projects share a concern for this issue that inevitably shows up in detailing and construction. They are not formally or ideologically modern or vernacular. Attempts to categorize them according to formal attributes or historical antecedents would diminish what they hold in common as contemporary works. Their essential and collective power lies in the degree to which they balance, and at some level accept, the demands placed on the house as a form of labor, a form of commodity, and a product that must accommodate the conflicting needs of developer and owner.

Seven Houses: Values

Architect	Project Status	Sales Price	Appraisal Value	Available Mortgage
Keith Krumwiede	not sold	$128,375	$111,000	$107,670
Morris Gutierrez	sold	$111,000	$107,000	$103,790
Carlos Jiménez	not sold	$105,929	$103,500	$100,395
Williams/Pizzini	not sold	$106,335	$98,000	$95,060
StudioWorks	not sold	$109,000	$106,000	$102,820
Lindy Roy	not sold	$129,000	$102,000	$98,940
Michael Bell	not sold	$118,000	$95,000	$87,300

Garden House by Morris Gutierrez Architects under construction

Lyons Village, a twenty-four unit, mixed-use apartment development designed and built by the FWCRC, as both developer and contractor, between 1998 and 2000

Contributors

StudioWorks received *Progressive Architecture* design awards in 1972, 1976, 1982, 1992, 1998, and 1999. **Robert Mangurian,** a principal of StudioWorks, received a B.Arch. from the University of California, Berkeley. He was a recipient of NEA grants in 1978, 1980, and 1992; the American Academy in Rome Collaborative Award with Vito Acconci in 1987; the Excellence in Teaching Award from the University of California, Los Angeles, in 1980 and 1982; and the NEA Mid-Career Fellowship at the American Academy in Rome in 1976–77. His publications include *Pamphlet Architecture 20: Seven Partly Underground Rooms and Buildings for Water, Ice, and Midgets,* 1997, with Mary-Ann Ray. **Mary-Ann Ray,** a principal of StudioWorks, received a B.F.A. from the University of Washington and an M.Arch. from Princeton University. She was a recipient of a Graham Foundation grant in 1998 and 1989; the Rome Prize Fellowship in 1987–88; the Howard Crosby Butler Traveling Fellowship, Bologna, in 1986; the Max Beckman Memorial Fellowship in 1981–82; and the Ford Foundation grant in 1979, 1980, and 1981. Her publications include *Lotus Special Document, "Dense City,"* which she edited with Roger Sherman in 1999.

Stanley Saitowitz is a professor of architecture at the University of California, Berkeley, and has taught at a number of schools including the Harvard University Design School, where he was Eliot Noyes Professor from 1991 to 1992, the University of Oklahoma, where he was Bruce Goff Professor in 1993, the Southern California Institute of Architecture, the University of California, Los Angeles, the University of Texas, Austin, and the University of the Witwatersrand. He has lectured extensively in the United States and abroad. Saitowitz's firm received the American Institute of Architects 1998 Henry Bacon Medal for Memorial Architecture and the Boston Society of Architects 1997 Harleston Parker Award.

Keith Krumwiede is the G. S. Wortham Assistant Professor of Architecture at Rice University and the principal of Standard. He received a B.A. from the University of California, Berkeley, and an M.Arch. from the Southern California Institute of Architecture.

Carol Treadwell was born in Oakland, California, in 1968. She and her sisters were raised in a series of seventeen separate-but-equal domiciles. In 1986, she graduated from Berkeley High School and, after some hedging, from the University of California, Berkeley, in 1991. Ever since, much to her pleasure and betterment, she has resided in the Los Angeles metropolitan area. Notably, she suffers from a nearly untempered addiction to sporting events of every description. Her cousins worry that she's too intellectual, but claim to like her anyway.

Brunner Pope Architects: Katrin Brunner is a principal at HOK, Houston, and a visiting professor at the University of Houston and the University of Texas, Austin. She received an M.Arch from the Southern California Institute of Architecture. **Albert Pope** is the Wortham Professor of Architecture at Rice University and the author of *Ladders.* His work has received numerous *Progressive Architecture* and American Institute of Architects design awards. He has taught at Rice University, the Yale University School of Architecture, and the Southern California Institute of Architecture, and is the founder of the Rice Center for Urbanism.

Carlos Jiménez moved to the United States in 1974, graduated from the College of Architecture at the University of Houston in 1981, and established Carlos Jiménez Studio in 1982. He is currently an associate professor at Rice University. He has been the McDermott Visiting Professor at the University of Texas, Austin, and the Eliot Noyes Visiting Professor at Harvard. In 2000, he served as a member of the jury for the Pritzker Architecture Prize. His work is the subject of several monographs, including *Carlos Jiménez* and *2G, Carlos Jiménez.*

TAFT Architects has received numerous awards, including three honor awards from the American Institute of Architects. The partners were awarded the 1985–1986 Advanced Fellowship in Architecture at the American Academy in Rome. In 1980 they were selected to represent the United States at the First International Exhibition of Architecture at the Venice Biennale. **John Casbarian**, FAIA, is a principal of TAFT Architects. He is a professor and associate dean at Rice University. Casbarian received a B.A. and a B.Arch. from Rice University, and an M.F.A. from the California Institute of the Arts. **Danny Samuels**, FAIA, is a principal of TAFT Architects. He received a B.A. and a B.Arch. from Rice University. Samuels is a visiting professor at Rice University and director of the Rice Building Workshop.

Nonya Grenader is a lecturer and visiting critic at Rice University and a fellow of the American Institute of Architects. Her work in affordable housing includes the design of a house for Project Row Houses in Houston, constructed with Danny Samuels and the Rice Building Workshop. Grenader's work has been published in *Texas Architect,* and she is a member of the editorial board at *Cite: The Architecture and Design Review of Houston.*

Lindy Roy teaches design at Princeton University and the Cooper Union Irwin S. Chanin School of Architecture. Before establishing her own firm in 1999, she worked with Peter Eisenman. She was the designer of the annual P.S.1 sculpture garden in 2001, and her work has been published extensively in journals such as *Assemblage.* She holds an M.Arch. from the Columbia University Graduate School of Architecture, Planning, and Preservation.

Morris Gutierrez Architects: Deborah Morris is an adjunct assistant professor of architecture and design at the University of Houston and has also taught at Rice University. A registered architect, she holds a B.F.A and an M.Arch. from the University of Texas, Austin. **Gabriella Gutierrez** is associate dean and associate professor at the University of New Mexico. She has also taught design at the University of Houston. Gutierrez holds an M.Arch. from Columbia University and was formerly in practice with Deborah Morris.

Natalye Appel is a fellow of the American Institute of Architects and has been recognized by the Houston Chapter of the American Institute of Architects with a Young Architect Award, acknowledging her commitment to the greater community through teaching, writing, and service. She has taught at Rice University, the University of Pennsylvania, the University of Houston, the University of Texas, and Texas A+M University. Her work has been published widely in the United States.

Trish Herrera was born Texas in 1954. She is a self-described subversive fiction writer with no apparent reason for bliss.

William Williams holds a B.Arch. from the University of Houston and is a graduate of the M.Arch. program at Harvard. He currently teaches at Rice University. His highly praised projects include a community center in East Oakland, California, a housing rehabilitation program for the City of Oakland, and the design and construction of a church in West Oakland. Williams has taught at the University of California, Berkeley, the University of California, Los Angeles, and the University of Virginia. His practice is based in Houston.

Archie Pizzini is an architect and artist based in Houston.

David Brown is an assistant professor at the Rice University School of Architecture. He is the author of a forthcoming book on the influence of jazz composition on modern architecture, and has also worked with Project Row Houses in Houston. He received a B.A. from Brown University and an M.Arch. from the University of California, Berkeley.

Bert Samples is an artist based in Houston. He is the founding director of the revitalized Lyons Avenue Theatre in Houston.

Lars Lerup is dean of the Rice University School of Architecture and author of *Building the Unfinished* and

After the City. His designs for architecture and furniture are included in the collections of the San Francisco Museum of Modern Art and the Canadian Centre for Architecture. Lerup's work has been published extensively in the United States and Europe. He is a fellow of the Rice Center for Urbanism.

Walter Hood is chair of the department of landscape architecture and associate professor in the urban design program at the University of California, Berkeley. He is the founder and principal of Hood Design, a landscape design practice in Oakland, California. Recent projects include the revitalization of downtown Oakland's venerable Lafayette Square Park, the adaptation of an abandoned railway corridor in East Oakland's Courtland Creek Park, and development work on San Francisco's Yerba Buena Lane, which will stretch between Market and Mission Streets and offer pedestrian access to Yerba Buena Gardens.

Thumb Design: Luke Bulman and **Kim Shoemake**, the principals, are visiting critics at the Rice University School of Architecture and have collaborated with Bruce Mau Design on numerous publication projects. They were design and production assistants for Lars Lerup and Sohela Faroki's installation room at the Menil Collection in Houston.

Sanford Kwinter is a New York–based writer who teaches design at the Rice University School of Architecture. Kwinter is the author of *Architectures of Time* and a founding editor of Zone Books. He is editor of *Zone 1/2, the Contemporary City* and *Zone 6, Incorporations*. He has taught at the Harvard University Design School, the Columbia University Graduate School of Architecture, the Parsons School of Design, and Rensselaer Polytechnic Institute. Kwinter collaborated with Rem Koolhaas and the Harvard Design School Project on the City on the exhibition and book *Mutations for the Arc en Rîve Centre dî Architecture*.

Bruce Mau founded his studio, Bruce Mau Design Inc. (BMD), in Toronto and designed *Zone 1/2* in 1985. Since then, BMD has gained international recognition for innovative, multidisciplinary work. Mau coauthored the critically acclaimed and award-winning *S,M,L,XL* with Rem Koolhaas. He is the recipient of the 1998 Chrysler Award for Design Innovation and the 1999 Toronto Arts Award for Architecture and Design.

Blair Satterfield, an associate and project designer at Bricker + Cannady Architects in Houston, and **Marc Swackhamer**, an assistant professor in the school of architecture and interior design at the University of Cincinnati, founded the firm Sleeve in 1998. Swackhamer recently coauthored *Ordinary Unfamiliarity: Foundation Pedagogy Through the Critique of the Everyday* with Kevin Klinger, which was presented at the Beginning Design conference at Portland State University, and collaborated with Terry Boling on the design of an installation for *Ecoventions*, an exhibition at the Cincinnati Contemporary Arts Center. Feedback House was published in volume two of the new periodical *306090*. Satterfield and Swackhamer are currently designing a building for Harris County Children's Protective Services and an urban park for the City of Conroe, in collaboration with BCA.

Ben Thorne is an associate of Interloop Architects. He is a graduate of the Yale University School of Architecture and the Rice University School of Architecture, and has worked in both photography and architecture. He was a project architect on the Live Oak Friends Meeting House in Houston with Leslie Elkins Architects and James Turrell, and has also worked on design and installations at the Water Mill Center with Robert Wilson. His photographs have been exhibited widely, most recently at the FotoFest annual exhibition in Houston.

Interloop Architects, a Houston-based architecture and design corporation, was founded in 1994 by **Mark Wamble**. Wamble has taught at Rice University, the Harvard University Design School, and the Columbia University Graduate School of Architecture. His awards include the *I.D.* design award honorable mention for the Klip Binder House; the *Progressive Architecture* design award for the renovation of Jones Plaza, Houston, with Bricker Cannady Architects; and the Young Architect Award from the Houston Chapter of the American Institute of Architects. He has been featured in the Young Architects program at the Architectural League of New York and the "40 Under 40" issue of *Interiors Magazine*. **Dawn Finley**, a principal of Interloop Architects, is an assistant professor of architecture at Rice University. She has published design and writing in *Perspecta*, the *Houston Press, Art Lies,* and *Architecture*. She has lectured at Yale University, Rice University, and the Museum of Fine Arts Houston.

In 1997, she joined Wamble at Interloop. They are currently at work on a collaboration with James Turrell and the Nasher Sculpture Center in Dallas for the Renzo Piano Building Workshop. Interloop's work has been shown at the Carnegie Museum of Art, the Milan Furniture Fair, the Kunsthal, and the *Rice-Nice* exhibition.

Michael Bell established Michael Bell Architecture in 1989. He is an associate professor of architecture and coordinator of the housing program at Columbia University; he is also codirector of the core design studios there. Bell has received four *Progressive Architecture* awards and citations. His projects have been shown at the Museum of Modern Art in New York, the Venice Biennale, the Yale University School of Architecture, and the University Art Museum at Berkeley, and are included in the permanent collection of the San Francisco Museum of Modern Art. Bell is the author of *Having Heard Mathematics* (Monacelli Press, 2003) and the editor, with Sze Tsung Leong, of *Slow Space* (Monacelli Press, 1998).

Chuihua Judy Chung is a partner with Sze Tsung Leong in a New York–based interdisciplinary practice that includes architecture, design, photography, editing, and writing. With Leong, she edited and designed the two-volume series on the complete works of Alison and Peter Smithson, *The Charged Void* (The Monacelli Press, 2001 and 2003), and is coeditor of *The Harvard Design School Guide to Shopping* and *Great Leap Forward* (Taschen, 2001). She will be teaching at Beijing University in 2004. She holds degrees from Smith College and Harvard University. **Sze Tsung Leong** is currently an associate professor of architecture at Beijing University. He is coeditor and designer of *Slow Space* (The Monacelli Press, 1998) and *The Harvard Design School Guide to Shopping* (Taschen, 2001). He holds degrees from the University of California, Berkeley, and Harvard University.

Deron Neblett graduated from Rice University in 1991 and launched Deron Neblett Photography in 1995. He has done editorial and documentary photography as well as commercial work, shooting hip hop, R&B, and rap artists for record labels and music publications. In 2000 he became the staff photographer for the *Houston Press*, a weekly news alternative. He has received numerous regional photojournalism and advertising awards.

Mardie Oakes graduated from the Rice University School of Architecture in 1996 and received an M.B.A. from Harvard Business School in 2002. For five years she was the lead project manager for the Fifth Ward Community Redevelopment Corporation in Houston. She is currently a service leadership fellow with Boston Community Capital, whose mission is to link low-income communities with the capital markets through lending and venture-capital investments. She sits on the boards of the ETC Development Corporation in Boston and the National Organization to Treat A-T, which raises money for research on the rare neurological disease that affects children.

Emily Todd received a B.A. in art and archaeology from Princeton University and an M.A. in art and art history from Rice University. She is currently a grant officer at Houston Endowment Inc., a philanthropy organization endowed by Mr. and Mrs. Jesse H. Jones. She was previously executive director of DiverseWorks Artspace in Houston, a nonprofit art center dedicated to presenting new visual, performing, and literary art (1995–99), and program director for the Andy Warhol Foundation for the Visual Arts, Inc., in New York (1988–95), and has worked in various curatorial positions on the staff of the Contemporary Arts Museum in Houston (1980–86). She is a member (and former board member) of ArtTable, an association of professional women in the arts, and a trustee of the Magnolia Charitable Trust.